THE WASHER OF THE FORD

LEGENDARY MORALITIES AND BARBARIC TALES

BY

FIONA MACLEOD

PROLOGUE

(TO KATHIA)

> *I find, under the boughs of love and hate, Eternal Beauty wandering on her way.*
>
> THE ROSE UPON THE ROOD OF TIME.

To you, in your far-away home in Provence, I send these tales out of the remote North you love so well, and so well understand. The same blood is in our veins, a deep current somewhere beneath the tide that sustains us. We have meeting-places that none knows of; we understand what few can understand; and we share in common a strange and inexplicable heritage. It is because you, who are called Kathia of the Sunway, are also Kathia nan Ciar, Kathia of the Shadow, it is because you are what you are that I inscribe this book to you. In it you will find much that is familiar to you, though you may never have read or heard anything of the kind; for there is a reality, beneath the unfamiliar accident, which may be recognised in a moment as native to the secret [4]life that lives behind the brain and the wise nerves with their dim ancestral knowledge.

The greater portion of this book deals with the remote life of a remote past. "The Shadow-Seers," however, though of to-day, may equally be of yesterday or to-morrow; and as for "The Last Supper" or "The Fisher of Men," they are of no time or date, for they are founded upon elemental facts which are modified but not transformed by the changing years.

It may be the last of its kind I shall write—at any rate, for a time. I would like it to be associated with you, to whom not only the mystery but the pagan sentiment and the old barbaric emotion are so near. With the second sight of the imagination we can often see more clearly in the perspectives of the past than in the maze of the present; and most clearly when we recognise that, below the accidents of time and circumstance, the present is but a reflection of that past to which we belong—belong, as intimately and inalienably, as to the hour wherein happily content we swing to those anchors which we do not see are linked to us by ropes of sand.

[5]If I am eager to have my say on other aspects of our Celtic life in the remoter West Highlands and in the Isles: now with the idyllic, now with the tragic, now with the grotesque, the humorous, the pathetic, with all the medley cast from the looms of Life—all that

> "... from the looms of Life are spun, Warp of shadow and woof of sun—"

and if, too, I long to express anew something of that wonderful historic romance in which we of our race and country are so rich, I am not likely to forget those earlier dreams which are no whit less realities—realities of the present seen through an inverted glass—which have been, and are, so full of inspiration and of a strange and terrible beauty.

But one to whom life appeals by a myriad avenues, all alluring and full of wonder and mystery, cannot always abide where the heart longs most to be. It is well to remember that there are shadowy waters even in the cities, and that the Fount of Youth is discoverable in the dreariest towns as well as in Hy Bràsil: a truth apt to be forgotten by those of us who dwell with ever-wondering [6]delight in that land of lost romance which had its own day, as this epoch of a still stranger, if a less obvious, romance has its own passing hour.

The titular piece—with its strange name that will not be unfamiliar to you who know our ancient Celtic literature, or may bear in mind the striking use made of it and its vague cognate legend, by Ferguson, in his Irish epic, *Congal*—gives the keynote not only of this book but of what has for hundreds of years, and to some extent still is, the characteristic of the purely Celtic mind in the Highlands and the Isles. This characteristic is a strange complexity of paganism and Christianity, or rather an apparent complexity arising from the grafting of Christianity upon paganism. Columba, St. Patrick, St. Ronan, Kentigern, all these militant Christian saints were merely transformed pagans. Even in the famous dialogue between St. Patrick and Oisìn, which is the folk-telling of the passing of the old before the new, the thrill of a pagan sympathy on the part of the uncompromising saint is unmistakable. To this day, there are [7]Christian rites and superstitions which are merely a gloss upon a surviving antique paganism. I have known an old woman, in no wise different from her neighbours, who on the day of Beltane sacrificed a hen: though for her propitiatory rite she had no warrant save that of vague traditional lore, the lore of the *teinntean*, of the hearth-side—where, in truth, are best to be heard the last echoes of the dim mythologic faith of our ancestors. What is the familiar "clachan," now meaning a hamlet with a kirk, but an echo of the Stones, the circles of the druids or of a more ancient worship still, that perhaps of the mysterious Anait, whose sole record is a *clach* on a lonely moor, of which from time immemorial the people have spoken as the "Teampull na'n Anait"? A relative of mine saw, in South Uist, less than twenty-five years ago, what may have been the last sun-sacrifice in Scotland, when an old Gael secretly and furtively slew a lamb on the summit of a conical grassy knoll at sunrise. Those who have the Gaelic have their ears filled with rumours of a day that is gone. When an evicted crofter laments, [8]*O mo chreach, mo chreach!*[1] or some poor soul on a bed of pain cries, *O mo chradshlat*,[2] he who knows the past recognises in the one the mournful refrain of the time when the sea-pirates or the hill-robbers pillaged and devasted quiet homesteads, and, in the other, not the moan of suffering only, but the cry of torment from the victim racked on the *cradhshlat*, a bitter ignominious torture used by the ancient Gaels. When, in good fellowship, one man says to another, *Tha, a laochain* (yes, my dear fellow), he recalls Fionn and the chivalry of eld, for *laochan* is merely a contraction for laoch-Fhinn, meaning a companion in war, a hero, literally

Fionn's right-hand man in battle. To this day, women, accompanying a marching regiment, are sometimes heard to say in the Gaelic, "We are going with the dear souls to the wars"—literally an echo of the Ossianic *Siubhlaidh sinn le'n anam do'n araich*, "We shall accompany their souls to the battle-field." A thousand instances could be [9]adduced. The language is a herring-net, through which the unchanging sea filtrates, even though the net be clogged with the fish of the hour. Nor is it the pagan atmosphere only that survives: often we breathe the air of that early day when the mind of man was attuned to a beautiful piety that was wrought into nature itself. Of the several words for the dawn, there is a beautiful one, *Uinneagachadh*. We have it in the phrase *'nuair a bha an latha ag uinneagachadh*, "when the day began to dawn." Now this word is simply an extension of *Uinneag*, a window: and the application of the image dates far back to the days of St. Columba, when some devout and poetic soul spoke of the *uinneagan Neimh*, the windows of Heaven.

> [1] Oh, alas, alas! (Literally, Oh, my undoing, or Oh, my utter ruin.)
>
> [2] Alas my torment!

Sometimes, among the innumerable "legendary moralities" which exist fragmentarily in the West Highlands and in the Isles, there is a coherent narrative basis—as, for example, in the Irish and Highland folk-lore about St. Bride, or Bridget, "Muime Chriosd." Sometimes there is simply a phrase survived out of antiquity. I doubt if any now living, either in the Hebrides or in Ireland, has heard any [10]legend of the "Washer of the Ford." The name survives, with its atmosphere of a remote past, its dim ancestral memory of a shadowy figure of awe haunting a shadowy stream in a shadowy land. Samuel Ferguson, in *Congal*, has done little more than limn an obscure shadow of that shadow: yet it haunts the imagination. In the passage of paganism, these old myths were too deep-rooted in the Celtic mind to vanish at the bidding of the Cross: thus came about that strange grafting of the symbolic imagery of the devout Culdee, of the visionary Mariolater, upon the surviving Druidic and prehistoric imagination. In a word, the Washer of the Ford might well have appeared, to a single generation, now as a terrible and sombre pagan goddess of death, now as a symbolic figure in the new faith, foreshadowing spiritual salvation and the mystery of resurrection.

If in a composition such as "The Annir-Choille," there is the expression of revolt—not ancient only, nor of the hour, but eternal, for the revolt is of the sovereign nature within us whereon all else is an accidental superstructure—against the Christian ethic of [11]renunciation, with an echo of our deep primeval longing for earth-kinship with every life in nature: if here there is the breath of a day that may not come again, there is little or nothing of the past, save what is merely accidental, in "The Fisher of Men" or "The Last Supper." I like to think that these *eachdaireachd Spioradail*, these spiritual chronicles, might as well, in substance, have been told a thousand years ago or be written a thousand years hence. That Fisher still haunts the invisible shadowy stream of human tears: those mystic Spinners still ply their triple shuttles, and the Fair Weaver of Hope, now as of yore and for ever, sends his rainbows adrift across the hearts and through the minds of men. What does it matter, again, that the Three Marvels of Hy are set against the background of the Iona of St. Columba? St. Francis blessed the birds of Assisi, and San Antonio had a heart as tender for all winged and gentle creatures: and there are innumerable quiet gardens of peace in the world even now where the kindred of San Antonio and St. Francis and St. Columba are kith to our fellow-beings, knowing them [12]akin one and all to the seals whom St. Molios blessed at the end of his days, and in his new humbleness hailed as likewise of the company of the Sons of God.

But of this I am sure. If there is spiritual truth in the vision of the Blind Harper who saw the Washer of the Ford, or in that of Molios who hailed the seals as brethren, or in that of Colum who blessed the birds and the fish of the sea and even the vagrant flies of the air, and saw the Moon-Child, and in that seeing learned the last mystery of the life of the soul, if in these, as in the "Fisher of Men" and "The Last Supper," I have given faint utterance to the heart-knowledge we all have, I would not have you or any think that the pagan way is therefore to me as the way of darkness. The lost monk who loved the Annir-Choille was doubtless not the less able to see the Uinneagan Neimh because he was under ban of Colum and all his kin: and there are those of us who would rather be with Cathal of the Woods, and be drunken with green fire, than gain the paradise of the holy Molios who banned him, if in that [13]gain were involved the forfeiture of the sunny green world, the joy of life, and the earth-sweet ancient song of the blood that is in the veins of youth.

These tales, let me add, are not legendary "mysteries" but legendary "moralities." They are reflections from the mirror that is often obscured but is never dimmed. There is no mystery in them, or anywhere: except the eternal mystery of beauty.

Of the Seanachas, the short barbaric tales, I will say nothing to you, whose favourite echo from Shelley is that thrilling line "the tempestuous loveliness of terror."

You in your far Provence, amid the austere hills that guard an ancient land of olive and vine, a land illumined by the blue flowing light of the Rhone, and girt by desert places where sun and wind inhabit, and scarce any other—you there and I here have this in common. Everywhere we see the life of man in subservient union with the life of Nature; never, in a word, as a sun beset by tributary stars, but as one planet among the innumerous concourse of the sky, nurtured, it may be, by light from other luminaries [14]and other spheres than we know of. That we are intimately at one with Nature is a cosmic truth we are all slowly approaching. It is not only the dog, it is not only the wild beast and the wood-dove, that are our close kindred, but the green tree and the green grass, the blue wave and the flowing wind, the flower of a day and the granite peak of an æon. And I for one would rather have the wind for comrade, and the white stars and green leaves as my kith and kin, than many a human companion, whose chief claim is the red blood that differs little from the sap in the grass or in the pines, and whose "deathless soul" is, mayhap, no more than a fugitive light blown idly for an hour betwixt dawn and dark. We are woven in one loom, and the Weaver thrids our being with the sweet influences, not only of the Pleiades, but of the living world of which each is no more than a multi-coloured thread: as, in turn, He thrids the wandering wind with the inarticulate cry, the yearning, the passion, the pain, of that bitter clan, the Human.

Truly, we are all one. It is a common [15]tongue we speak, though the wave has its own whisper, and the wind its own sigh, and the lip of the man its word, and the heart of woman its silence.

Long, long ago a desert king, old and blind, but dowered with ancestral wisdom beyond all men that have lived, heard that the Son of God was born among men. He rose from his place, and on the eve of the third day he came to where Jesus sat among the gifts brought by the wise men of the East. The little lad sat in Mary's lap, beneath a tree filled with quiet light; and while the folk of Bethlehem came and went He was only a child as other children are. But when the desert king drew near, the child's eyes deepened with knowledge.

"What is it, my little son?" said Mary the Virgin.

"Sure, Mother dear," said Jesus, who had never yet spoken a word, "it is Deep Knowledge that is coming to me."

"And what will that be, O my Wonder and Glory?"

"That which will come in at the door before you speak to me again."

[16]Even as the child spoke, an old blind man entered, and bowed his head.

"Come near, O tired old man," said Mary that had borne a son to Joseph, but whose womb knew him not.

With that the tears fell into the old man's beard. "Sorrow of Sorrows," he said, "but that will be the voice of the Queen of Heaven!"

But Jesus said to his mother: "Take up the tears, and throw them into the dark night." And Mary did so: and lo! upon the wilderness, where no light was, and on the dark wave, where seamen toiled without hope, clusters of shining stars rayed downward in a white peace.

Thereupon the old king of the desert said:

"Heal me, O King of the Elements."

And Jesus healed him. His sight was upon him again, and his gray ancientness was green youth once more.

"I have come with Deep Knowledge," he said.

"Ay, sure, I am for knowing that," said the King of the Elements, that was a little child.

[17]"Well, if you will be knowing that, you can tell me who is at my right side?"

"It is my elder brother the Wind."

"And what colour will the Wind be?"

"Now blue as Hope, now green as Compassion."

"And who is on my left?"

"The Shadow of Life."

"And what colour will the Shadow be?"

"That which is woven out of the bowels of the earth and out of the belly of the sea."

"Truly, thou art the King of the Elements. I am bringing you a great gift, I am: I have come with Deep Knowledge."

And with that the old blind man, whose eyes were now as stars, and whose youth was a green garland about him, chanted nine runes.

The first rune was the Rune of the Four Winds.

The second rune was the Rune of the Deep Seas.

The third rune was the Rune of the Lochs and Rivers and the Rains and the Dews and the many waters.

[18]The fourth rune was the Rune of the Green Trees and of all things that grow.

The fifth rune was the Rune of Man and Bird and Beast, and of everything that lives and moves, in the air, on the earth, and in the sea: all that is seen of man, and all that is unseen of man.

The sixth rune was the Rune of Birth, from the spawn on the wave to the Passion of Woman.

The seventh rune was the Rune of Death, from the quenching of a gnat to the fading of the stars.

The eighth rune was the Rune of the Soul that dieth not, and the Spirit that is.

The ninth rune was the Rune of the Mud and the Dross and the Slime of Evil —that is the Garden of God, wherein He walks with sunlight streaming from the palms of his hands and with stars springing beneath his feet.

Then when he had done, the old man said: "I have brought you Deep Knowledge." But at that Jesus the Child said:

"All this I heard on my way hither."

The old desert king bowed his head. [19]Then he took a blade of grass, and played upon it. It was a wild, strange air that he played.

"Iosa mac Dhe, tell the woman what song *that* is," cried the desert king.

"It is the secret speech of the Wind that is my Brother," cried the child, clapping his hands for joy.

"And what will this be?" and with that the old man took a green leaf, and played a lovely whispering song.

"It is the secret speech of the leaves," cried Jesus the little lad, laughing low.

And thereafter the desert king played upon a handful of dust, and upon a drop of water, and upon a flame of fire; and the Child laughed for the knowing and the joy. Then he gave the secret speech of the singing bird, and the barking fox, and the howling wolf, and the bleating sheep: of all and every created kind.

"O King of the Elements," he said then, "for sure you knew much; but now I have made you to know the secret things of the green Earth that is Mother of you and of Mary too."

[20]But while Jesus pondered that one mystery, the old man was gone: and when he got to his people, they put him alive into a hollow of the earth and covered him up, because of his shining eyes, and the green youth that was about him as a garland.

And when Christ was nailed upon the Cross, Deep Knowledge went back into the green world, and passed into the grass and the sap in trees, and the flowing wind, and the dust that swirls and is gone.

All this is of the wisdom of the long ago, and you and I are of those who know how ancient it is, how remoter far than when Mary, at the bidding of her little son, threw up into the firmament the tears of an old man.

It is old, old—

> "Thousands of years, thousands of years,If all were told."

Is it wholly unwise, wholly the fantasy of a dreamer, to insist, in this late day, when the dust behind and the mist before hide from [21]us the Beauty of the World, that we can regain our birthright only by leaving our cloud-palaces of the brain, and becoming consciously at one with the cosmic life of which, merely as men, we are no more than a perpetual phosphorescence?

[25]

THE WASHER OF THE FORD

WHEN Torcall the Harper heard of the death of his friend, Aodh-of-the-Songs, he made a vow to mourn for him for three seasons—a green time, an apple time, and a snow time.

There was sorrow upon him because of that death. True, Aodh was not of his kindred, but the singer had saved the harper's life when his friend was fallen in the Field of Spears.

Torcall was of the people of the north—of the men of Lochlin. His song was of the fjords, and of strange gods, of the sword and the war-galley, of the red blood and the white breast, of Odin and Thor and Freya, of Balder and the Dream-God that sits in the rainbow, of the starry North, of the flames of pale blue and flushing rose that play around the Pole, of sudden death in battle, and of Valhalla.

[26] Aodh was of the south isles, where these shake under the thunder of the western seas. His clan was of the isle that is now called Barra, and was then Iondû; but his mother was a woman out of a royal rath in Banba, as men of old called Eiré. She was so fair that a man died of his desire of her. He was named Ulad, and was a prince. "The Melancholy of Ulad" was long sung in his land after his end in the dark swamp, where he heard a singing, and went laughing glad to his death. Another man was made a prince because of her. This was Aodh the Harper, out of the Hebrid Isles. He won the heart out of her, and it was his from the day she heard his music and felt his eyes flame upon her. Before the child was born, she said, "He shall be the son of love. He shall be called Aodh. He shall be called Aodh-of-the-Songs." And so it was.

Sweet were his songs. He loved, and he sang, and he died.

And when Torcall that was his friend knew this sorrow, he arose and made his vow, and went out for evermore from the place where he was.

[27] Since the hour of the Field of Spears he had been blind. Torcall Dall he was upon men's lips thereafter. His harp had a moonshine wind upon it from that day, it was said: a beautiful strange harping when he went down through the glen, or out upon the sandy machar by the shore, and played what the wind sang, and the grass whispered, and the tree murmured, and the sea muttered or cried hollowly in the dark.

Because there was no sight to his eyes, men said he saw and he heard. What was it he heard and he saw that they saw not and heard not? It was in the voice that was in the strings of his harp, so the rumour ran.

When he rose and went away from his place, the Maormor asked him if he went north, as the blood sang; or south, as the heart cried; or west, as the dead go; or east, as the light comes.

"I go east," answered Torcall Dall.

"And why so, Blind Harper?"

"For there is darkness always upon me, and I go where the light comes."

On that night of the nights, a fair wind [28]blowing out of the west, Torcall the Harper set forth in a galley. It splashed in the moonshine as it was rowed swiftly by nine men.

"Sing us a song, O Torcall Dall!" they cried.

"Sing us a song, Torcall of Lochlin," said the man who steered. He and all his company were of the Gael: the Harper only was of the Northmen.

"What shall I sing?" he asked. "Shall it be of war that you love, or of women that twine you like silk o' the kine; or shall it be of death that is your meed; or of your dread, the Spears of the North?"

A low sullen growl went from beard to beard.

"We are under *geas*, Blind Harper," said the steersman, with downcast eyes because of his flaming wrath; "we are under bond to take you safe to the mainland, but we have sworn no vow to sit still under the lash of your tongue. 'Twas a wind-fleet arrow that sliced the sight out of your eyes: have a care lest a sudden sword-wind sweep the breath out of your body."

[29]Torcall laughed a low, quiet laugh.

"Is it death I am fearing now—I who have washed my hands in blood, and had love, and known all that is given to man? But I will sing you a song, I will."

And with that he took his harp, and struck the strings.

> There is a lonely stream afar in a lone dim land:It hath white dust for shore it has, white bones bestrew the strand:The only thing that liveth there is a naked leaping sword;But I, who a seer am, have seen the whirling handOf the Washer of the Ford.
> A shadowy shape of cloud and mist, of gloom and dusk, she stands,The Washer of the Ford:She laughs, at times, and strews the dust through the hollow of her hands.
> She counts the sins of all men there, and slays the red-stained horde—The ghosts of all the sins of men must know the whirling swordOf the Washer of the Ford.

> She stoops and laughs when in the dust she sees a writhing limb:
> "Go back into the ford," she says, "and hither and thither swim;
> [30]Then I shall wash you white as snow, and shall take you by the hand,
> And slay you here in the silence with this my whirling brand,
> And trample you into the dust of this white windless sand—"
> This is the laughing word
> Of the Washer of the Ford
> Along that silent strand.

There was silence for a time after Torcall Dall sang that song. The oars took up the moonshine and flung it hither and thither like loose shining stones. The foam at the prow curled and leaped.

Suddenly one of the rowers broke into a long, low chant—

> *Yo, eily-a-ho, ayah-a-ho, eily-ayah-a-ho,*
> Singeth the Sword
> *Eily-a-ho, ayah-a-ho, eily-ayah-a-ho,*
> Of the Washer of the Ford!

And at that all ceased from rowing. Standing erect, they lifted up their oars against the stars, and the wild voices of them flew out upon the night—

> *Yo, eily-a-ho, ayah-a-ho, eily-ayah-a-ho,*
> Singeth the Sword
> *Eily-a-ho, ayah-a-ho, eily-ayah-a-ho,*
> Of the Washer of the Ford!

[31]Torcall Dall laughed. Then he drew his sword from his side and plunged it into the sea. When he drew the blade out of the water and whirled it on high, all the white shining drops of it swirled about his head like a sleety rain.

And at that the steersman let go the steering-oar and drew his sword, and clove a flowing wave. But with the might of his blow the sword spun him round, and the sword sliced away the ear of the man who had the sternmost oar. Then there was blood in the eyes of all there. The man staggered, and felt for his knife, and it was in the heart of the steersman.

Then because these two men were leaders, and had had a blood-feud, and because all there, save Torcall, were of one or the other side, swords and knives sang a song.

The rowers dropped their oars; and four men fought against three.

Torcall laughed, and lay back in his place. While out of the wandering wave the death of each man clambered into the hollow of the boat, and breathed its chill upon its man, Torcall the Blind took his harp. He sang [32]this song, with the swirling spray against his face, and the smell of blood in his nostrils, and the feet of him dabbling in the red tide that rose there.

> Oh, 'tis a good thing the red blood, by Odin his word!And a good thing it is to hear it bubbling deep.And when we hear the laughter of the Sword,Oh, the corbies croak, and the old wail, and the women weep!And busy will she be there where she stands,Washing the red out of the sins of all this slaying horde;And trampling the bones of them into white powdery sands,And laughing low at the thirst of her thirsty sword—The Washer of the Ford!

When he had sung that song there was only one man whose pulse still beat, and he was at the bow.

"A bitter black curse upon you, Torcall Dall!" he groaned out of the ooze of blood that was in his mouth.

"And who will you be?" said the Blind Harper.

"I am Fergus, the son of Art, the son of Fergus of the Dûns."

[33]"Well, it is a song for your death I will make, Fergus mac Art mhic Fheargus: and because you are the last."

With that Torcall struck a wild sob out of his harp, and he sang—

> Oh, death of Fergus, that is lying in the boat here,Betwixt the man of the red hair and him of the black beard,Rise now, and out of thy cold white eyes take out the fear,And let Fergus mac Art mhic Fheargus see his weird!
>> Sure, now, it's a blind man I am, but I'm thinking I seeThe shadow of you crawling across the dead.Soon you will twine your arm around his shaking knee,And be whispering your silence into his listless head.And that is why, O Fergus—

But here the man hurled his sword into the sea, and with a choking cry fell forward; and upon the white sands he was, beneath the trampling feet of the Washer of the Ford.

[34]

II

It was a fair wind that blew beneath the stars that night. At dawn the mountains of Skye were like turrets of a great Dûn against the east.

But Torcall the Blind Harper did not see that thing. Sleep, too, was upon him. He smiled in that sleep, for in his mind he saw the dead men, that were of the alien people, his foes, draw near the stream that was in a far place. The shaking of them, poor, tremulous frostbit leaves they were, thin and sere, made the only breath there was in that desert.

At the ford—this is what he saw in his vision—they fell down like stricken deer with the hounds upon them.

"What is this stream?" they cried in the thin voice of rain across the moors.

"The River of Blood," said a voice.

"And who are you that are in the silence?"

"I am the Washer of the Ford."

And with that each red soul was seized and thrown into the water of the ford; and [35]when white as a sheep-bone on the hill, was taken in one hand by the Washer of the Ford and flung into the air, where no wind was and where sound was dead, and was then severed this way and that, in four whirling blows of the sword from the four quarters of the world. Then it was that the Washer of the Ford trampled upon what fell to the ground, till under the feet of her was only a white sand, white as powder, light as the dust of the yellow flowers that grow in the grass.

It was at that Torcall Dall smiled in his sleep. He did not hear the washing of the sea; no, nor any idle plashing of the unoared boat. Then he dreamed, and it was of the woman he had left, seven summer-sailings ago, in Lochlin. He thought her hand was in his, and that her heart was against his.

"Ah, dear, beautiful heart of woman," he said, "and what is the pain that has put a shadow upon you?"

It was a sweet voice that he heard coming out of sleep.

"Torcall, it is the weary love I have."

[36]"Ah, heart o' me, dear! sure 'tis a bitter pain I have had, too, and I away from you all these years."

"There's a man's pain, and there's a woman's pain."

"By the blood of Balder, Hildyr, I would have both upon me to take it off the dear heart that is here."

"Torcall!"

"Yes, white one."

"We are not alone, we two in the dark."

And when she had said that thing, Torcall felt two baby arms go round his neck, and two leaves of a wild rose press cool and sweet against his lips.

"Ah! what is this?" he cried, with his heart beating, and the blood in his body singing a glad song.

A low voice crooned in his ear: a bitter-sweet song it was, passing-sweet, passing-bitter.

"Ah, white one, white one," he moaned; "ah, the wee fawn o' me! Baby o' foam, bonnie wee lass, put your sight upon me that I may see the blue eyes that are mine too and Hildyr's."

[37]But the child only nestled closer. Like a fledgling in a great nest she was. If God heard her song, He was a glad God that day. The blood that was in her body called to the blood that was in his body. He could say no word. The tears were in his blind eyes.

Then Hildyr leaned into the dark, and took his harp, and played upon it. It was of the fonnsheen he had learned, far, far away, where the isles are.

She sang: but he could not hear what she sang.

Then the little lips, that were like a cool wave upon the dry sand of his life, whispered into a low song: and the wavering of it was like this in his brain—

> Where the winds gather
> The souls of the dead,
> O Torcall, my father,
> My soul is led!
>> In Hildyr-mead
>> I was thrown, I was sown:
>> Out of thy seed
>> I am sprung, I am blown!
>> But where is the way
>> For Hildyr and me,
>> By the hill-moss gray
>> Or the gray sea?
>> For a river is here,
>> And a whirling sword—
>> And a Woman washing
>> By a Ford!

With that, Torcall Dall gave a wild cry, and sheathed an arm about the wee white one, and put out a hand to the bosom that loved him. But there was no white breast there, and no white babe: and what was against his lips was his own hand red with blood.

"O Hildyr!" he cried.

But only the splashing of the waves did he hear.

"O white one!" he cried.

But only the scream of a sea-mew, as it hovered over that boat filled with dead men, made answer.

III

All day the Blind Harper steered the galley of the dead. There was a faint wind moving out of the west. The boat went before it, slow, and with a low, sighing wash.

Torcall saw the red gaping wounds of the dead, and the glassy eyes of the nine men.

"It is better not to be blind and to see the dead," he muttered, "than to be blind and to see the dead."

The man who had been steersman leaned against him. He took him in his shuddering grip and thrust him into the sea.

But when, an hour later, he put his hand to the coolness of the water, he drew it back with a cry, for it was on the cold, stiff face of the dead man that it had fallen. The long hair had caught in a cleft in the leather where the withes had given.

For another hour Torcall sat with his chin in his right hand, and his unseeing eyes staring upon the dead. He heard no sound at all, save the lap of wave upon wave, and the [40]*suss* of spray against spray, and a bubbling beneath the boat, and the low, steady swish of the body that trailed alongside the steering oar.

At the second hour before sundown he lifted his head. The sound he heard was the sound of waves beating upon rocks.

At the hour before sundown he moved the oar rapidly to and fro, and cut away the body that trailed behind the boat. The noise of the waves upon the rocks was now a loud song.

When the last sunfire burned upon his neck and made the long hair upon his shoulders ashine, he smelt the green smell of grass. Then it was too that he heard the muffled fall of the sea, in a quiet haven, where shelves of sand were.

He followed that sound, and while he strained to hear any voice the boat grided upon the sand, and drifted to one side. Taking his harp, Torcall drove an oar into the sand, and leaped on to the shore. When he was there, he listened. There was silence. Far, far away he heard the falling of a mountain-torrent, and the thin, faint cry of [41]an eagle, where the sun-flame dyed its eyrie as with streaming blood.

So he lifted his harp, and, harping low, with a strange, wild song on his lips, moved away from that place, and gave no more thought to the dead.

It was deep gloaming when he came to a wood. He felt the cold green breath of it.

"Come," said a voice, low and sweet.

"And who will *you* be?" asked Torcall the Harper, trembling because of the sudden voice in the stillness.

"I am a child, and here is my hand, and I will lead you, Torcall of Lochlin."

The blind man had fear upon him.

"Who are you that in a strange place are for knowing who I am?"

"Come."

"Ay, sure, it is coming I am, white one; but tell me who you are, and whence you came, and whither we go."

Then a voice that he knew sang:

> O where the winds gather
> The souls of the dead,
> O Torcall, my father,
> My soul is led!
>
> [42]But a river is here,
> And a whirling Sword—
> And a Woman washing
> By a Ford!

Torcall Dall was as the last leaf on a tree at that.

"Were you on the boat?" he whispered hoarsely.

But it seemed to him that another voice answered: "*Yea, even so.*"

"Tell me, for I have blindness: Is it peace?"

"It is peace."

"Are you man, or child, or of the Hidden People?"

"I am a shepherd."

"A shepherd? Then, sure, you will guide me through this wood? And what will be beyond this wood?"

"A river."

"And what river will that be?"

"Deep and terrible. It runs through the Valley of the Shadow."

"And is there no ford there?"

"Ay, there is a ford."

"And who will guide me across that ford?"

[43]"She."

"Who?"

"The Washer of the Ford."

But hereat Torcall Dall gave a sore cry and snatched his hand away, and fled sidelong into an alley of the wood.

It was moonshine when he lay down, weary. The sound of flowing water filled his ears.

"Come," said a voice.

So he rose and went. When the cold breath of the water was upon his face, the guide that led him put a fruit into his hand.

"Eat, Torcall Dall!"

He ate. He was no more Torcall Dall. His sight was upon him again. Out of the blackness shadows came; out of the shadows, the great boughs of trees; from the boughs, dark branches and dark clusters of leaves; above the branches, white stars; below the branches, white flowers; and beyond these, the moonshine on the grass and the moonfire on the flowing of a river dark and deep.

"Take your harp, O Harper, and sing the song of what you see."

[44] Torcall heard the voice, but saw no one. No shadow moved. Then he walked out upon the moonlit grass; and at the ford he saw a woman stooping and washing shroud after shroud of woven sunbeams: washing them there in the flowing water, and singing a low song that he did not hear. He did not see her face. But she was young, and with long black hair that fell like the shadow of night over a white rock.

So Torcall took his harp, and he sang:

> Glory to the great Gods, it is no Sword I am seeing:Nor do I see aught but the flowing of a river.And I see shadows on the flow that are ever fleeing,And I see a woman washing shrouds for ever and ever.

Then he ceased, for he heard the woman sing:

> Glory to God on high, and to Mary, Mother of Jesus,Here am I washing away the sins of the shriven,O Torcall of Lochlin, throw off the red sins that ye cherishAnd I will be giving you the washen shroud that they wear in Heaven.

Filled with a great awe, Torcall bowed his head. Then once more he took his harp, and he sang:

> [45] O well it is I am seeing, Woman of the Shrouds,That you have not for me any whirling of the Sword:I have lost my gods, O woman, so what will the name beOf thee and thy gods, O woman that art Washer of the Ford?

But the woman did not look up from the dark water, nor did she cease from washing the shrouds made of the woven moonbeams. But he heard this song above the sighing of the water:

> It is Mary Magdalene my name is, and I loved Christ.And Christ is the son of God, and Mary the Mother of Heaven.And this river is the river of death, and the shadowsAre the fleeing souls that are lost if they be not shriven.

Then Torcall drew nigher unto the stream. A melancholy wind was upon it.

"Where are all the dead of the world?" he said.

But the woman answered not.

"And what is the end, you that are called Mary?"

Then the woman rose.

"Would you cross the Ford, O Torcall the Harper?"

He made no word upon that. But he listened. He heard a woman singing faint and low far away in the dark. He drew more near.

"Would you cross the Ford, O Torcall?"

He made no word upon that. But once more he listened. He heard a little child crying in the night.

"Ah, lonely heart of the white one," he sighed, and his tears fell.

Mary Magdalene turned and looked upon him.

It was the face of Sorrow she had. She stooped and took up the tears. "They are bells of joy," she said. And he heard a wild sweet ringing in his ears.

A prayer came out of his heart. A blind prayer it was, but God gave it wings. It flew to Mary, who took and kissed it, and gave it song.

"It is the Song of Peace," she said. And Torcall had peace.

"What is best, O Torcall?" she asked, rustling-sweet as rain among the leaves her voice was—"What is best? The sword, or peace?"

"Peace," he answered: and he was white now, and was old.

"Take your harp," Mary said, "and go in unto the Ford. But lo, now I clothe you with a white shroud. And if you fear the drowning flood, follow the bells that were your tears: and if the dark affright you, follow the song of the Prayer that came out of your heart."

So Torcall the Harper moved into the whelming flood, and he played a wild strange air, like the laughing of a child.

Deep silence there was. The moonshine lay upon the obscure wood, and the darkling river flowed sighing through the soundless gloom. The Washer of the Ford stooped once more. Low and sweet, as of yore and for ever, over the drowning souls, she sang her immemorial song.

[49]

MUIME CHRIOSD

[50]Note.—This "legendary romance" is based upon the ancient and still current (though often hopelessly contradictory) legends concerning Brighid, or Bride, commonly known as "Muime Chriosd," that is, the Foster-Mother of Christ. From the universal honour and reverence in which she was and is held—second only in this respect to the Virgin herself—she is also called "Mary of the Gael." Another name, frequent in the West, is "Brighde-nam-Brat," that is, St. Bride of the Mantle, a name explained in the course of my legendary story. Brighid the Christian saint should not, however, as is commonly done, be confused with a much earlier and remoter Brighid, the ancient Celtic muse of Song.

[51]

ST. BRIDE OF THE ISLES

SLOINNEADH BRIGHDE, MUIME CHRIOSD

> Brighde nighean Dùghaill Duinn,'Ic Aoidth, 'ic Arta, 'ic Cuinn.Gach la is gach oidhcheNi mi cuimhneachadh air sloinneadh Brighde.Cha mharbhar mi,Cha ghuinear mi,Cha ghonar mi,Cha mho dh' fhagas Criosd an dearmad mi;Cha loisg teine gniomh Shatain mi;'S cha bhath uisge no saile mi;'S mi fo chomraig Naoimh Moire'S mo chaomh mhuime, Brighde.

THE GENEALOGY OF ST. BRIDGET OR ST. BRIDE, FOSTER-MOTHER OF CHRIST.

St. Bridget, the daughter of Dùghall Donn,Son of Hugh, son of Art, son of Conn.Each day and each nightI will meditate on the genealogy of St. Bridget.[Whereby] I will not be killed,I will not be wounded,I will not be bewitched;Neither will Christ forsake me;[52]Satan's fire will not burn me;Neither water nor sea shall drown me;For I am under the protection of the Virgin Mary,And my meek and gentle foster-mother, St. Bridget.

I

BEFORE ever St. Colum came across the Moyle to the island of Iona, that was then by strangers called Innis-nan-Dhruidhneach, the Isle of the Druids, and by the natives Ioua, there lived upon the southeast slope of Dun-I a poor herdsman, named Dùvach. Poor he was, for sure, though it was not for this reason that he could not win back to Ireland, green Banba, as he called it: but because he was an exile thence, and might never again smell the heather blowing over Sliabh-Gorm in what of old was the realm of Aoimag.

He was a prince in his own land, though none on Iona save the Arch-Druid knew what his name was. The high priest, however, knew that Dùvach was the royal Dùghall, called Dùghall Donn, the son of Hugh the King, the son of Art, the son of [53]Conn. In his youth he had been accused of having done a wrong against a noble maiden of the blood. When her child was born he was made to swear across her dead body that he would be true to the daughter for whom she had given up her life, that he would rear her in a holy place but away from Eiré, and that he would never set foot within that land again. This was a bitter thing for Dùghall Donn to do: the more so as, before the King, and the priests, and the people, he swore by the Wind, and by the Moon, and by the Sun, that he was guiltless of the thing of which he was accused. There were many there who believed him because of that sacred oath: others, too, forasmuch as that Morna the Princess had herself sworn to the same effect. Moreover, there was Aodh of the Golden Hair, a poet and seer, who avowed that Morna had given birth to an immortal, whose name would one day be as a moon among the stars for glory. But the King would not be appeased, though he spared the life of his youngest son. So it was that, by the advice of Aodh of the Druids, Dùghall Donn went northwards [54]through the realm of Clanadon and so to the sea-loch that was then called Loch Feobal. There he took boat with some wayfarers bound for Alba. But in the Moyle a tempest arose, and the frail galley was driven northward, and at sunrise was cast like a great fish, spent and dead, upon the south end of Ioua, that is now Iona. Only two of the mariners survived: Dùghall Donn and the little child. This was at the place where, on a day of the days in a year that was not yet come, St. Colum landed in his coracle, and gave thanks on his bended knees.

When, warmed by the sun, they rose, they found themselves in a waste place. Ill was Dùghall in his mind because of the portents, and now to his astonishment and alarm the child Bridget knelt on the stones, and, with claspt hands, small and pink as the sea-shells round about her, sang a song of words which were unknown to him. This was the more marvellous, as she was yet but an infant, and could say no word even of Erse, the only tongue she had heard.

At this portent, he knew that Aodh had [55]spoken seeingly. Truly this child was not of human parentage. So he, too, kneeled, and, bowing before her, asked if she were of the race of the Tuatha de Danann, or of the older gods, and what her will was, that he might be her servant. Then it was that the kneeling babe looked at him, and sang in a low sweet voice in Erse:

> I am but a little child,Dùghall, son of Hugh, son of Art,But my garment shall be laidOn the lord of the world,Yea, surely it shall be that HeThe King of the Elements HimselfShall lean against my bosom,And I will give him peace,And peace will I give to all who askBecause of this mighty Prince,And because of his Mother that is the Daughter of Peace.

And while Dùghall Donn was still marvelling at this thing, the Arch-Druid of Iona approached, with his white-robed priests. A grave welcome was given to the stranger, but while the youngest of the servants of God was entrusted with the child, the Arch-Druid took Dùghall aside, and questioned [56]him. It was not till the third day that the old man gave his decision. Dùghall Donn was to abide on Iona if he so willed: the child certainly was to stay. His life would be spared, nor would he be a bondager of any kind, and a little land to till would be given him, and all that he might need. But of his past he was to say no word. His name was to become as naught, and he was to be known simply as Dùvach. The child, too, was to be named Bride, for that was the way the name Bridget was called in the Erse of the Isles.

To the question of Dùghall, that was thenceforth Dùvach, as to why he laid so great stress on the child, that was a girl, and the reputed offspring of shame at that, Cathal the Arch-Druid replied thus: "My kinsman Aodh of the Golden Hair, who sent you here, was wiser than Hugh the King and all the Druids of Aoimag. Truly, this child is an Immortal. There is an ancient prophecy concerning her: surely of her who is now here, and no other. There shall be, it says, a spotless maid born of a virgin of the ancient immemorial race in Innisfail. [57]And when for the seventh time the sacred year has come, she will hold Eternity in her lap as a white flower. Her maiden breasts shall swell with milk for the Prince of the World. She shall give suck to the King of the Elements. So I say unto you, Dùvach, go in peace. Take unto thyself a wife, and live upon the place I will give thee on the east side of Ioua. Treat Bride as though she were thy spirit, but leave her much alone, and let her learn of the sun and the wind. In the fulness of time the prophecy shall be fulfilled."

So was it, from that day of the days. Dùvach took a wife unto himself, who weaned the little Bride, who grew in beauty and grace, so that all men marvelled. Year by year for seven years the wife of Dùvach bore him a son, and these grew apace in strength, so that by the beginning of the third year of the seventh cycle of Bride's life there were three stalwart youths to brother her, and three comely and strong lads, and one young boy fair to see. Nor did any one, not even Bride herself, saving Cathal the Arch-Druid, know that Dùvach [58]the herdsman was Dùghall Donn, of a princely race in Innisfail.

In the end, too, Dùvach came to think that he had dreamed, or at the least that Cathal had not interpreted the prophecy aright. For though Bride was of exceeding beauty, and of a strange piety that made the young Druids bow before her as though she were a bàndia, yet the world went on as before, and the days brought no change. Often, while she was still a child, he had questioned her about the words she had said as a babe, but she had no memory of them. Once, in her ninth year, he came upon her on the hillside of Dun-I singing these selfsame words. Her eyes dreamed afar away. He bowed his head, and, praying to the Giver of light, hurried to Cathal. The old man bade him speak no more to the child concerning the mysteries.

Bride lived the hours of her days upon the slopes of Dun-I, herding the sheep, or in following the kye upon the green hillocks and grassy dunes of what then as now was called the Machar. The beauty of the world was her daily food. The spirit within her [59]was like sunlight behind a white flower. The birdeens in the green bushes sang for joy when they saw her blue eyes. The tender prayers that were in her heart for all the beasts and birds, for helpless children, and tired women, and for all who were old, were often seen flying above her head in the form of white doves of sunshine.

But when the middle of the year came that was, though Dùvach had forgotten it, the year of the prophecy, his eldest son, Conn, who was now a man, murmured against the virginity of Bride, because of her beauty and because a chieftain of the mainland was eager to wed her. "I shall wed Bride or raid Ioua" was the message he had sent.

So one day, before the great fire of the summer festival, Conn and his brothers reproached Bride.

"Idle are these pure eyes, O Bride, not to be as lamps at thy marriage-bed."

"Truly, it is not by the eyes that we live," replied the maiden gently, while to their fear and amazement she passed her hand before her face and let them see that the sockets [60]were empty. Trembling with awe at this portent, Dùvach intervened.

"By the Sun I swear it, O Bride, that thou shalt marry whomsoever thou wilt and none other, and when thou willest, or not at all if such be thy will."

And when he had spoken, Bride smiled, and passed her hand before her face again, and all there were abashed because of the blue light as of morning that was in her shining eyes.

II

The still weather had come, and all the isles lay in beauty. Far south, beyond vision, ranged the coasts of Eiré: westward, leagues of quiet ocean dreamed into unsailed wastes whose waves at last laved the shores of Tirna'n Òg, the Land of Eternal Youth: northward, the spell-bound waters sparkled in the sunlight, broken here and there by purple shadows, that were the isles of Staffa and Ulva, Lunga and the isles of the columns, misty Coll, and Tiree that is the land beneath the wave; with, pale blue in the heat-haze, [61]the mountains of Rùm called Haleval, Haskeval, and Oreval, and the sheer Scuir-na-Gillian and the peaks of the Cuchullins in remote Skye.

All the sweet loveliness of a late spring remained, to give a freshness to the glory of summer. The birds had song to them still.

It was while the dew was yet wet on the grass that Bride came out of her father's house, and went up the steep slope of Dun-I. The crying of the ewes and lambs at the pastures came plaintively against the dawn. The lowing of the kye arose from the sandy hollows by the shore, or from the meadows on the lower slopes. Through the whole island went a rapid trickling sound, most sweet to hear: the myriad voices of twittering birds, from the dotterel in the sea-weed to the larks climbing the blue spirals of heaven.

This was the morning of her birth, and she was clad in white. About her waist was a girdle of the sacred rowan, the feathery green leaves of it flickering dusky shadows upon her robe as she moved. The light upon her yellow hair was as when morning wakes, laughing low with joy amid the tall corn. As [62]she went she sang, soft as the crooning of a dove. If any had been there to hear he would have been abashed, for the words were not in Erse, and the eyes of the beautiful girl were as those of one in a vision.

When, at last, a brief while before sunrise, she reached the summit of the Scuir, that is so small a hill and yet seems so big in Iona where it is the sole peak, she found three young Druids there, ready to tend the sacred fire the moment the sun-rays should kindle it. Each was clad in a white robe, with fillets of oak-leaves; and each had a golden armlet. They made a quiet obeisance as she approached. One stepped forward, with a flush in his face because of her beauty, that was as a sea-wave for grace, and a flower for purity, and sunlight for joy, and moonlight for peace, and the wind for fragrance.

"Thou mayst draw near if thou wilt, Bride, daughter of Dùvach," he said, with something of reverence as well as of grave courtesy in his voice: "for the holy Cathal hath said that the Breath of the Source of All is upon thee. It is not lawful for women to be here at this moment, but thou hast the law shining upon [63]thy face and in thine eyes. Hast thou come to pray?"

But at that moment a low cry came from one of his companions. He turned, and rejoined his fellows. Then all three sank upon their knees, and with outstretched arms hailed the rising of God.

As the sun rose, a solemn chant swelled from their lips, ascending as incense through the silent air. The glory of the new day came soundlessly. Peace was in the blue heaven, on the blue-green sea, on the green land. There was no wind, even where the currents of the deep moved in shadowy purple. The sea itself was silent, making no more than a sighing slumber-breath round the white sands of the isle, or a hushed whisper where the tide lifted the long weed that clung to the rocks.

In what strange, mysterious way, Bride did not see; but as the three Druids held their hands before the sacred fire there was a faint crackling, then three thin spirals of blue smoke rose, and soon dusky red and wan yellow tongues of flame moved to and fro. The sacrifice of God was made. Out of the immeasurable heaven He had come, in His [64]golden chariot. Now, in the wonder and mystery of His love, He was reborn upon the world, reborn a little fugitive flame upon a low hill in a remote isle. Great must be His love that He could die thus daily in a thousand places: so great His love that He could give up His own body to daily death, and suffer the holy flame that was in the embers he illumined to be lighted and revered and then scattered to the four quarters of the world.

Bride could bear no longer the mystery of this great love. It moved her to an ecstasy. What tenderness of divine love that could thus redeem the world daily: what long-suffering for all the evil and cruelty done hourly upon the weeping earth, what patience with the bitterness of the blind fates! The beauty of the worship of Be'al was upon her as a golden glory. Her heart leaped to a song that could not be sung. The inexhaustible love and pity in her soul chanted a hymn that was heard of no Druid or mortal anywhere, but was known of the white spirits of Life.

Bowing her head, so that the glad tears [65]fell warm as thunder-rain upon her hands, she rose and moved away.

Not far from the summit of Dun-I is a hidden pool, to this day called the Fountain of Youth. Hitherward she went, as was her wont when upon the hill at the break of day, at noon, or at sundown. Close by the huge boulder, which hides it from above, she heard a pitiful bleating, and soon the healing of her eyes was upon a lamb which had become fixed in a crevice in the rock. On a crag above it stood a falcon, with savage cries, lusting for warm blood. With swift step Bride drew near. There was no hurt to the lambkin as she lifted it in her arms. Soft and warm was it there, as a young babe against the bosom that mothers it. Then with quiet eyes she looked at the falcon, who hooded his cruel gaze.

"There is no wrong in thee, Seobhag," she said gently; "but the law of blood shall not prevail for ever. Let there be peace this morn."

And when she had spoken this word, the wild hawk of the hills flew down upon her shoulder, nor did the heart of the lambkin [66]beat the quicker, while with drowsy eyes it nestled as against its dam. When she stood by the pool she laid the little woolly creature among the fern. Already the bleating of it was sweet against the forlorn heart of a ewe. The falcon rose, circled above her head, and with swift flight sped through the blue air. For a time Bride watched its travelling shadow: when it was itself no more than a speck in the golden haze, she turned, and stooped above the Fountain of Youth.

Beyond it stood then, though for ages past there has been no sign of either, two quicken-trees. Now they were gold-green in the morning light, and the brown-green berries that had not yet reddened were still small. Fair to see was the flickering of the long finger-shadows upon the granite rocks and boulders.

Often had Bride dreamed through their foliage; but now she stared in amaze. She had put her lips to the water, and had started back because she had seen, beyond her own image, that of a woman so beautiful that her soul was troubled within her, and had cried its inaudible cry, worshipping. When, [67]trembling, she had glanced again, there was none beside herself. Yet what had happened? For, as she stared at the quicken-trees, she saw that their boughs had interlaced, and that they now became a green arch. What was stranger still was that the rowan-clusters hung in blood-red masses, although the late heats were yet a long way off.

Bride rose, her body quivering because of the cool sweet draught of the Fountain of Youth, so that almost she imagined the water was for her that day what it could be once in each year to every person who came to it, a breath of new life and the strength and joy of youth. With slow steps she advanced towards the arch of the quickens. Her heart beat as she saw that the branches at the summit had formed themselves into the shape of a wreath or crown, and that the scarlet berries dropped therefrom a steady rain of red drops as of blood. A sigh of joy breathed from her lips when, deep among the red and green, she saw the white merle of which the ancient poets sang, and heard the exceeding wonder of its rapture, which was now the pain of joy and now the joy of pain.

The song of the mystic bird grew wilder and more sweet as she drew near. For a brief while she hesitated. Then, as a white dove drifted slow before her under and through the quicken-boughs, a dove white as snow but radiant with sunfire, she moved forward to follow, with a dream-smile upon her face and her eyes full of the sheen of wonder and mystery, as shadowy waters flooded with moonshine.

And this was the passing of Bride, who was not seen again of Dùvach or her foster-brothers for the space of a year and a day. Only Cathal, the aged Arch-Druid, who died seven days thence, had a vision of her, and wept for joy.

III

When the strain of the white merle ceased, though it had seemed to her scarce longer than the vanishing song of the swallow on the wing, Bride saw that the evening was come. Through the violet glooms of dusk she moved soundlessly, save for the crispling of her feet among the hot sands. Far as she could see to right or left there were hollows and ridges of sand; where, here and there, trees or shrubs grew out of the parched soil, they were strange to her. She had heard the Druids speak of the sunlands in a remote, nigh unreachable East, where there were trees called palms, trees in a perpetual sunflood yet that perished not, also tall dark cypresses, black-green as the holy yew. These were the trees she now saw. Did she dream, she wondered? Far down in her mind was some memory, some floating vision only, mayhap, of a small green isle far among the northern seas. Voices, words, faces, familiar yet unfamiliar when she strove to bring them near, haunted her.

The heat brooded upon the land. The sigh of the parched earth was "Water, water."

As she moved onward through the gloaming she descried white walls beyond her: white walls and square white buildings, looming ghostly through the dark, yet home-sweet as the bells of the cows on the sea-pastures, because of the yellow lights every here and there agleam.

[70]A tall figure moved towards her, clad in white, even as those figures which haunted her unremembering memory. When he drew near she gave a low cry of joy. The face of her father was sweet to her.

"Where will be the pitcher, Brighid?" he said, though the words were not the words that were near her when she was alone. Nevertheless she knew them, and the same manner of words was upon her lips.

"My pitcher, father?"

"Ah, dreamer, when will you be taking heed! It is leaving your pitcher you will be, and by the Well of the Camels, no doubt: though little matter will that be, since there is now no water, and the drought is heavy upon the land. But ... Brighid ..."

"Yes, my father?"

"Sure now it is not safe for you to be on the desert at night. Wild beasts come out of the darkness, and there are robbers and wild men who lurk in the shadow. Brighid ... Brighid ... is it dreaming you are still?"

"I was dreaming of a cool green isle in northern seas, where ..."

"Where you have never been, foolish lass, [71]and are never like to be. Sure, if any wayfarer were to come upon us you would scarce be able to tell him that yonder village is Bethlehem, and that I am Dùghall Donn the inn-keeper, Dùghall the son of Hugh, son of Art, son of Conn. Well, well, I am growing old, and they say that the old see wonders. But I do not wish to see this wonder, that my daughter Brighid forgets her own town, and the good inn that is there, and the strong sweet ale that is cool against the thirst of the weary. Sure, if the day of my days is near it is near. 'Green be the place of my rest,' I cry, even as Oisìn the son of Fionn of the hero-line of Trenmor cried in his old age; though if Oisìn and the Fiànn were here not a green place would they find now, for the land is burned dry as the heather after a hill-fire. But now, Brighid, let us go back into Bethlehem, for I have that for the saying which must be said at once."

In silence the twain walked through the gloaming that was already the mirk, till they came to the white gate, where the asses and camels breathed wearily in the sultry darkness, with dry tongues moving round parched mouths. Thence they fared through narrow streets, where a few white-robed Hebrews and sons of the desert moved silently, or sat in niches. Finally, they came to a great yard, where more than a score of camels lay huddled and growling in their sleep. Beyond this was the inn, which was known to all the patrons and friends of Dùghall Donn as the "Rest and Be Thankful," though formerly as the Rest of Clan-Ailpean, for was he not himself through his mother MacAlpine of the Isles, as well as blood-kin to the great Carmac the Ard-Righ, to whom his father, Hugh, was feudatory prince?

As Dùghall and Bride walked along the stone flags of a passage leading to the inner rooms, he stopped and drew her attention to the water-tanks.

"Look you, my lass," he said sorrowfully, "of these tanks and barrels nearly all are empty. Soon there will be no water whatever, which is an evil thing though I whisper it in peace, to the Stones be it said. Now, already the folk who come here murmur. No man can drink ale all day long, and those wayfarers who want to wash the dust of their journey from their feet and hands complain bitterly. And ... what is that you will be saying? The kye? Ay, sure, there is the kye, but the poor beasts are o'ercome with the heat, and there's not a Cailliach on the hills who could win a drop more of milk from them than we squeeze out of their udders now, and that only with rune after rune till all the throats of the milking lassies are as dry as the salt grass by the sea.

"Well, what I am saying is this: 'tis months now since any rain will be falling, and every crock of water has been for the treasuring as though it had been the honey of Moy-Mell itself. The moon has been full twice since we had the good water brought from the mountain-springs; and now they are for drying up too. The seers say that the drought will last. If that is a true word, and there be no rain till the winter comes, there will be no inn in Bethlehem called 'The Rest and Be Thankful;' for already there is not enough good water to give peace even to your little thirst, my birdeen. As for the ale, it is poor drink now for man or maid, and as for the camels and asses, poor beasts, they don't understand the drinking of it."

"That is true, father; but what is to be done?"

"That's what I will be telling you, my lintie. Now, I have been told by an oganach out of Jerusalem, that lives in another place close by the great town, that there is a quenchless well of pure water, cold as the sea with a north wind in it, on a hill there called the Mount of Olives. Now, it is to that hill I will be going. I am for taking all the camels, and all the horses, and all the asses, and will lade each with a burthen of water-skins, and come back home again with water enough to last us till the drought breaks."

That was all that was said that night. But at the dawn the inn was busy, and all the folk in Bethlehem were up to see the going abroad of Dùghall Donn and Ronald M'Ian, his shepherd, and some Macleans and Maccallums that were then in that place. It was a fair sight to see as they went forth through the white gate that is called the Gate of Nazareth. A piper walked first, playing the [75]Gathering of the Swords: then came Dùghall Donn on a camel, and M'Ian on a horse, and the herdsmen on asses, and then there were the collies barking for joy.

Before he had gone, Dùghall took Bride out of the hearing of the others. There was only a little stagnant water, he said; and as for the ale, there was no more than a flagon left of what was good. This flagon, and the one jar of pure water, he left with her. On no account was she to give a drop to any wayfarer, no matter how urgent he might be; for he, Dùghall, could not say when he would get back, and he did not want to find a dead daughter to greet him on his return, let alone there being no maid of the inn to attend to customers. Over and above that, he made her take an oath that she would give no one, no, not even a stranger, accommodation at the inn, during his absence.

Afternoon and night came, and dawn and night again, and yet again. It was on the afternoon of the third day, when even the crickets were dying of thirst, that Bride heard a clanging at the door of the inn.

When she went to the door she saw a [76]weary gray-haired man, dusty and tired. By his side was an ass with drooping head, and on the ass was a woman, young, and of a beauty that was as the cool shadow of green leaves and the cold ripple of running waters. But beautiful as she was, it was not this that made Bride start: no, nor the heavy womb that showed the woman was with child. For she remembered her of a dream—it was a dream, sure—when she had looked into a pool on a mountain-side, and seen, beyond her own image, just this fair and beautiful face, the most beautiful that ever man saw since Nais, of the Sons of Usna, beheld Deirdrê in the forest,—ay, and lovelier far even than she, the peerless among women.

"Gu'm beannaicheadh Dia an tigh," said the gray-haired man in a weary voice, "the blessing of God on this house."

"Soraidh leat," replied Bride gently, "and upon you likewise."

"Can you give us food and drink, and, after that, good rest at this inn? Sure it is grateful we will be. This is my wife Mary, upon whom is a mystery: and I am Joseph, a carpenter in Arimathea."

[77]"Welcome, and to you, too, Mary: and peace. But there is neither food nor drink here, and my father has bidden me give shelter to none who comes here against his return."

The carpenter sighed, but the fair woman on the ass turned her shadowy eyes upon Bride, so that the maiden trembled with joy and fear.

"And is it forgetting me you will be, Brighid-Alona," she murmured, in the good sweet Gaelic of the Isles, and the voice of her was like the rustle of leaves when a soft rain is falling in a wood.

"Sure, I remember," Bride whispered, filled with deep awe. Then without a word she turned, and beckoned them to follow: which, having left the ass by the doorway, they did.

"Here is all the ale that I have," she said, as she gave the flagon to Joseph: "and here, Mary, is all the water that there is. Little there is, but it is you that are welcome to it."

Then, when they had quenched their thirst she brought out oatcakes and scones and brown bread, and would fain have added milk, but there was none.

"Go to the byre, Brighid," said Mary, "and the first of the kye shall give milk."

So Bride went, but returned saying that the creature would not give milk without a sian or song, and that her throat was too dry to sing.

"Say this *sian*," said Mary:—

> Give up thy milk to her who callsAcross the low green hills of HeavenAnd stream-cool meads of Paradise!

And sure enough, when Bride did this, the milk came: and she soothed her thirst, and went back to her guests rejoicing. It was sorrow to her not to let them stay where they were, but she could not, because of her oath.

The man Joseph was weary, and said he was too tired to seek far that night, and asked if there was no empty byre or stable where he and Mary could sleep till morning. At that, Bride was glad: for she knew there was a clean cool stable close to the byre where her kye were: and thereto she led them, and returned with peace at her heart.

When she was in the inn again, she was afraid once more: for lo, though Mary and Joseph had drunken deep of the jar and the flagon, each was now full as it had been. Of the food, too, none seemed to have been taken, though she had herself seen them break the scones and the oatcakes.

It was dusk when her reverie was broken by the sound of the pipes. Soon thereafter Dùghall Donn and his following rode up to the inn, and all were glad because of the cool water, and the grapes, and the green fruits of the earth, that they brought with them.

While her father was eating and drinking, merry because of the ale that was still in the flagon, Bride told him of the wayfarers. Even as she spoke, he made a sign of silence, because of a strange, unwonted sound that he heard.

"What will that be meaning?" he asked, in a low, hushed voice.

"Sure it is the rain at last, father. That is a glad thing. The earth will be green again. The beasts will not perish. Hark, I hear the noise of it coming down from the hills as well." But Dùghall sat brooding.

"Aye," he said at last, "is it not foretold that the Prince of the World is to be born in [80]this land, during a heavy falling of rain, after a long drought? And who is for knowing that Bethlehem is not the place, and that this is not the night of the day of the days? Brighid, Brighid, the woman Mary must be the mother of the Prince, who is to save all mankind out of evil and pain and death!"

And with that he rose and beckoned to her to follow. They took a lantern, and made their way through the drowsing camels and asses and horses, and past the byres where the kye lowed gently, and so to the stable.

"Sure that is a bright light they are having," Dùghall muttered uneasily: for, truly, it was as though the shed were a shell filled with the fires of sunrise.

Lightly they pushed back the door. When they saw what they saw they fell upon their knees. Mary sat with her heavenly beauty upon her like sunshine on a dusk land: in her lap, a Babe laughing sweet and low.

Never had they seen a Child so fair. He was as though wrought of light.

[81]"Who is it?" murmured Dùghall Donn, of Joseph, who stood near, with rapt eyes.

"It is the Prince of Peace."

And with that Mary smiled, and the Child slept.

"Brighid, my sister dear"—and, as she whispered this, Mary held the little one to Bride.

The fair girl took the Babe in her arms, and covered it with her mantle. Therefore it is that she is known to this day as Brighde-nam-Brat, St. Bride of the Mantle.

And all through that night, while the mother slept, Bride nursed the Child, with tender hands and croodling crooning songs. And this was one of the songs that she sang:

> Ah, Baby Christ, so dear to me,Sang Bridget Bride:How sweet thou art,My baby dear,Heart of my heart!
>> Heavy her body was with thee,Mary, beloved of One in Three,Sang Bridget Bride—Mary, who bore thee, little lad:But light her heart was, light and gladWith God's love clad.
>> [82]Sit on my knee,Sang Bridget Bride:Sit hereO Baby dear,Close to my heart, my heart:For I thy foster-mother am,My helpless lamb!O have no fear,Sang good St. Bride.
>> None, none,No fear have I:So let me clingClose to thy sideWhilst thou dost sing,O Bridget Bride!
>> My Lord, my Prince I sing:My baby dear, my King!Sang Bridget Bride.

It was on this night that, far away in Iona, the Arch-Druid Cathal died. But before the breath went from him he had his vision of joy, and his last words were:

> Brighde 'dol air a glùn,Righ nan dùl a shuidh 'na h-uchd!
> (Bridget Bride upon her knee,The King of the Elements asleep on her breast!)

[83]At the coming of dawn Mary awoke, and took the Child. She kissed Bride upon the brows, and said this thing to her: "Brighid, my sister dear, thou shalt be known unto all time as Muime Chriosd."

IV

No sooner had Mary spoken than Bride fell into a deep sleep. So profound was this slumber that when Dùghall Donn came to see to the wayfarers, and to tell them that the milk and the porridge were ready for the breaking of their fast, he could get no word of her at all. She lay in the clean, yellow straw beneath the manger, where Mary had laid the Child. Dùghall stared in amaze. There was no sign of the mother, nor of the Babe that was the Prince of Peace, nor of the douce, quiet man that was Joseph the carpenter. As for Bride, she not only slept so sound that no word of his fell against her ears, but she gave him awe. For as he looked at her he saw that she was surrounded by a glowing light. Something in his heart [84]shaped itself into a prayer, and he knelt beside her, sobbing low. When he rose, it was in peace. Mayhap an angel had comforted his soul in its dark shadowy haunt of his body.

It was late when Bride awoke, though she did not open her eyes, but lay dreaming. For long she thought she was in Tir-Tairngire, the Land of Promise, or wandering on the honey-sweet plain of Magh-Mell; for the wind of dreamland brought exquisite odours to her, and in her ears was a most marvellous sweet singing.

All round her there was a music of rejoicing. Voices, lovelier than any she had ever heard, resounded; glad voices full of praise and joy. There was a pleasant tumult of harps and trumpets, and as from across blue hills and over calm water came the sound of the bagpipes. She listened with tears. Loud and glad were the pipes, at times full of triumph, as when the heroes of old marched with Cuculain or went down to battle with Fionn: again, they were low and sweet, like humming of bees when the heather is heavy with the honey-ooze. The songs and wild [85]music of the angels lulled her into peace: for a time no thought of the woman Mary came to her, nor of the Child that was her foster-child.

Suddenly it was in her mind as though the pipes played the chant that is called the "Aoibhneas a Shlighe," "the joy of his way," a march played before a bridegroom going to his bride. Out of this glad music came a solitary voice, like a child singing on the hillside.

"The way of wonder shall be thine, O Brighid-Naomha!"

This was what the child-voice sang. Then it was as though all the harpers of the west were playing "air clàrsach": and the song of a multitude of voices was this:

"Blessed art thou, O Brighid, who nursed the King of the Elements in thy bosom: blessed thou, the Virgin Sister of the Virgin Mother, for unto all time thou shalt be called Muime Chriosd, the Foster-Mother of Jesus that is the Christ."

With that, Bride remembered all, and opened her eyes. Naught strange was there to see, save that she lay in the stable. Then [86]as she noted that the gloaming had come, she wondered at the soft light that prevailed in the shed, though no lamp or candle burned there. In her ears, too, still lingered a wild and beautiful music.

It was strange. Was it all a dream, she pondered. But even as she thought thus, she saw half of her mantle lying upon the straw in the manger. Much she marvelled at this, but when she took the garment in her hand she wondered more. For though it was no more than a half of the poor mantle wherewith she had wrapped the Babe, it was all wrought with mystic gold lines and with precious stones more glorious than ever Arch-Druid or Island Prince had seen. The marvel gave her awe at last, when, as she placed the garment upon her shoulder, it covered her completely.

She knew now that she had not dreamed, and that a miracle was done. So with gladness she went out of the stable, and into the inn. Dùghall Donn was amazed when he saw her, and then rejoiced exceedingly.

"Why are you so merry, my father?" she asked.

[87]"Sure it is glad that I am. For now the folk will be laughing the wrong way. This very morning I was so pleased with the pleasure, that while the pot was boiling on the peats I went out and told every one I met that the Prince of Peace was come, and had just been born in the stable behind the 'Rest and Be Thankful.' Well, that saying was just like a weasel among the rabbits, only it was an old toothless weasel: for all Bethlehem mocked me, some with jeers, some with hard words, and some with threats. Sure, I cursed them right and left. No, not for all my cursing—and by the blood of my fathers, I spared no man among them, wishing them sword and fire, the black plague and the gray death—would they believe. So back it was that I came, and going through the inn I am come to the stable. 'Sorrow is on me like a gray mist,' said Oisìn, mourning for Oscur, and sure it was a gray mist that was on me when not a sign of man, woman, or child was to be seen, and you so sound asleep that a March gale in the Moyle wouldn't have roused you. Well, I went back and told this thing, and all the [88]people in Bethlehem mocked at me. And the Elders of the People came at last, and put a fine upon me: and condemned me to pay three barrels of good ale, and a sack of meal, and three thin chains of gold, each three yards long: and this for causing a false rumour, and still more for making a laughing-stock of the good folk of Bethlehem. There was a man called Murdoch-Dhu, who is the chief smith in Nazareth, and it's him I'm thinking will have laughed the Elders into doing this hard thing."

It was then that Bride was aware of a marvel upon her, for she blew an incantation off the palm of her hand, and by that frith she knew where the dues were to be found.

"By what I see in the air that is blown off the palm of my hand, father, I bid you go into the cellar of the inn. There you will find three barrels full of good ale, and beside them a sack of meal, and the sack is tied with three chains of gold, each three yards long."

But while Dùghall Donn went away rejoicing, and found that which Bride had foretold, she passed out into the street. None [89]saw her in the gloaming, or as she went towards the Gate of the East. When she passed by the Lazar-house she took her mantle off her back and laid it in the place of offerings. All the jewels and fine gold passed into invisible birds with healing wings: and these birds flew about the heads of the sick all night, so that at dawn every one arose, with no ill upon him, and went on his way rejoicing. As each went out of Bethlehem that morning of the mornings he found a clean white robe and new sandals at the first mile; and, at the second, food and cool water; and, at the third, a gold piece and a staff.

The guard that was at the Eastern Gate did not hail Bride. All the gaze of him was upon a company of strange men, shepherd-kings, who said they had come out of the East led by a star. They carried rare gifts with them when they first came to Bethlehem: but no man knew whence they came, what they wanted, or whither they went.

For a time Bride walked along the road that leads to Nazareth. There was fear in her gentle heart when she heard the howling [90]of hyenas down in the dark hollows, and she was glad when the moon came out and shone quietly upon her.

In the moonlight she saw that there were steps in the dew before her. She could see the black print of feet in the silver sheen on the wet grass, for it was on a grassy hill that she now walked, though a day ago every leaf and sheath there had lain brown and withered. The footprints she followed were those of a woman and of a child.

All night through she tracked those wandering feet in the dew. They were always fresh before her, and led her away from the villages, and also where no wild beasts prowled through the gloom. There was no weariness upon her, though often she wondered when she should see the fair wondrous face she sought. Behind her also were footsteps in the dew, though she knew nothing of them. They were those of the Following Love. And this was the Lorgadh-Brighde of which men speak to this day: the Quest of the holy St. Bride.

All night she walked; now upon the high slopes of a hill. Never once did she have a [91]glimpse of any figure in the moonlight, though the steps in the dew before her were newly made, and none lay in the glisten a short way ahead.

Suddenly she stopped. There were no more footprints. Eagerly she looked before her. On a hill beyond the valley beneath her she saw the gleaming of yellow stars. These were the lights of a city. "Behold, it is Jerusalem," she murmured, awe-struck, for she had never seen the great town.

Sweet was the breath of the wind that stirred among the olives on the mount where she stood. It had the smell of heather, and she could hear the rustle of it among the bracken on a hill close by.

"Truly, this must be the Mount of Olives," she whispered. "The Mount of which I have heard my father speak, and that must be the hill called Calvary."

But even as she gazed marvelling, she sighed with new wonder; for now she saw that the yellow stars were as the twinkling of the fires of the sun along the crest of a hill that is set in the east. There was a living joy in the dawntide. In her ears was a [92]sweet sound of the bleating of ewes and lambs. From the hollows in the shadows came the swift singing rush of the flowing tide. Faint cries of the herring gulls filled the air; from the weedy boulders by the sea the skuas called wailingly.

Bewildered, she stood intent. If only she could see the footprints again, she thought. Whither should she turn, whither go? At her feet was a yellow flower. She stooped and plucked it.

"Tell me, O little sun-flower, which way shall I be going?" and as she spoke a small golden bee flew up from the heart of it, and up the hill to the left of her. So it is that from that day the dandelion is called am-Bèarnàn-Bhrighde.

Still she hesitated. Then a sea-bird flew by her with a loud whistling cry.

"Tell me, O eisireùn," she called, "which way shall I be going?"

And at this the eisireùn swerved in its flight, and followed the golden bee, crying, "This way, O Bride, Bride, Bride, Bride, Bri-i-i-ide!"

So it is that from that day the [93]oyster-catcher has been called the Gille-Brighde, the Servant of St. Bridget.

Then it was that Bride said this sian:

> Dia romham;Moire am dheaghuidh;'S am Mac a thug Righ nan Dul!Mis' air do shlios, a Dhia,Is Dia ma'm luirg.Mac' 'oire, a's Righ nan Dul,A shoillseachadh gach ni dheth so,Le a ghras, mu'm choinneamh.
>> God before me;The Virgin Mary after me;And the Son sent by the King of the Elements.I am to windward of thee, O God!And God on my footsteps.May the Son of Mary, King of the Elements,Reveal the meaning of each of these thingsBefore me, through His grace.

And as she ended she saw before her two quicken-trees, of which the boughs were interwrought so that they made an arch. Deep in the green foliage was a white merle that sang a wondrous sweet song. Above it the small branches were twisted into the shape of a wreath or crown, lovely with the [94]sunlit rowan-clusters, from whose scarlet berries red drops as of blood fell.

Before her flew a white dove, all aglow as with golden light.

She followed, and passed beneath the quicken arch.

Sweet was the song of the merle, that was then no more; sweet the green shadow of the rowans, that now grew straight as young pines. Sweet the far song in the sky, where the white dove flew against the sun.

Bride looked, and her eyes were glad. Bonnie the blooming of the heather on the slopes of Dun-I. Iona lay green and gold, isled in her blue waters. From the sheiling of Dùvach, her father, rose a thin column of pale blue smoke. The collies, seeing her, barked loudly with welcoming joy.

The bleating of the sheep, the lowing of the kye, the breath of the salt wind from the open sea beyond, the song of the flowing tide in the Sound beneath: dear the homing.

With a strange light in her eyes she moved down through the heather and among the green bracken: white, wonderful, fair to see.

THE FISHER OF MEN

"But now I have grown nothing, being all, And the whole world weighs down upon my heart."

FERGUS AND THE DRUID.

WHEN old Sine nic Leòid came back to the croft, after she had been to the burn at the edge of the green airidh, where she had washed the *claar* that was for the potatoes at the peeling, she sat down before the peats.

She was white with years. The mountain wind was chill, too, for all that the sun had shone throughout the midsummer day. It was well to sit before the peat-fire.

The croft was on the slope of a mountain, and had the south upon it. North, south, east, and west, other great slopes reached upward, like hollow green waves frozen into silence by the very wind that curved them so, and freaked their crests into peaks and jagged pinnacles. Stillness was in that place for ever and ever. What though the Gorromalt Water foamed down Ben Nair, where the croft was, and made a hoarse voice for aye surrendering sound to silence? What though at times the stones fell from the ridges of Ben Chaisteal and Maolmòr, and clattered down the barren declivities till they were slung in the tangled meshes of whin and juniper? What though on stormy dawns the eagle screamed as he fought against the wind that graved a thin line upon the aged front of Ben Mulad, where his eyrie was: or that the kestrel cried above the rabbit-burrows in the strath: or that the hill-fox barked, or that the curlew wailed, or that the scattered sheep made an endless mournful crying? What were these but the ministers of silence?

There was no blue smoke in the strath except from the one turf cot. In the hidden valley beyond Ben Nair there was a hamlet, and nigh upon three-score folk lived there: but that was over three miles away. Sine Macleod was alone in that solitary place, save for her son Alasdair Mòr Òg. "Young Alasdair" he was still, though the gray feet of fifty years had marked his hair. Alasdair Òg he was while Alasdair Ruadh mac Chalum mhic Leòid, that was his father, lived. But when Alasdair Ruadh changed, and Sine was left a [99]mourning woman, he that was their son was Alasdair Òg still.

She had sore weariness that day. For all that, it was not the weight of the burden that made her go in out of the afternoon sun, and sit by the red glow of the peats, brooding deep.

When, nigh upon an hour later, Alasdair came up the slope and led the kye to the byre, she did not hear him: nor had she sight of him, when his shadow flickered in before him and lay along the floor.

"Poor old woman," he said to himself, bending his head because of the big height that was his, and he there so heavy and strong, and tender, too, for all the tangled black beard and the wild hill-eyes that looked out under bristling gray-black eyebrows.

"Poor old woman, and she with the tired heart that she has. Ay, ay, for sure the weeks lap up her shadow, as the sayin' is. She will be thinking of him that is gone. Ay, or maybe the old thoughts of her are goin' back on their own steps, down this glen an' over that hill an' away beyont that [100]strath, an' this corrie an' that moor. Well, well, it is a good love, that of the mother. Sure a bitter pain it will be to me when there's no old gray hair there to stroke. It's quiet here, terrible quiet, God knows, to Himself be the blessin' for this an' for that: but when she has the white sleep at last, then it'll be a sore day for me, an' one that I will not be able to bear to hear the sheep callin', callin', callin' through the rain on the hills here, and Gorromalt Water an' no other voice to be with me on that day of the days."

She heard a faint sigh, and stirred a moment, but did not look round.

"Muim'-à-ghraidh, is it tired you are, an' this so fine a time, too?"

With a quick gesture, the old woman glanced at him.

"Ah, child, is that you indeed? Well, I am glad of that, for I have the trouble again."

"What trouble, Muim'-ghaolaiche?"

But the old woman did not answer. Wearily she turned her face to the peat-glow again.

Alasdair seated himself on the big wooden chair to her right. For a time he stayed [101]silent thus, staring into the red heart of the peats. What was the gloom upon the old heart that he loved? What trouble was it?

At last he rose and put meal and water into the iron pot, and stirred the porridge while it seethed and sputtered. Then he poured boiling water upon the tea in the brown jenny, and put the new bread and the sweet-milk scones on the rude deal board that was the table.

"Come, dear tired old heart," he said, "and let us give thanks to the Being."

"Blessings and thanks," she said, and turned round.

Alasdair poured out the porridge, and watched the steam rise. Then he sat down, with a knife in one hand and the brown-white loaf in the other.

"O God," he said, in the low voice he had in the kirk when the bread and wine were given—"O God, be giving us now thy blessing, and have the thanks. And give us peace."

Peace there was in the sorrowful old eyes of the mother. The two ate in silence. The big clock that was by the bed *tick-tacked*, *tick-tacked*. A faint sputtering came out of [102]a peat that had bog-gas in it. Shadows moved in the silence, and met and whispered and moved into deep, warm darkness. There was peace.

There was still a red flush above the hills in the west when the mother and son sat in the ingle again.

"What is it, mother-my-heart?" Alasdair asked at last, putting his great red hand upon the woman's knee.

She looked at him for a moment. When she spoke she turned away her gaze again.

"Foxes have holes, and the fowls of the air have their places of rest, but the Son of Man hath not where to lay his head."

"And what then, dear? Sure, it is the deep meaning you have in that gray old head that I'm loving so."

"Ay, lennav-aghray, there is meaning to my words. It is old I am, and the hour of my hours is near. I heard a voice outside the window last night. It is a voice I will not be hearing, no, not for seventy years. It was cradle-sweet, it was."

She paused, and there was silence for a time.

"Well, dear," she began again, wearily, and in a low, weak voice, "it is more tired and more tired I am every day now this last month. Two Sabbaths ago I woke, and there were bells in the air: and you are for knowing well, Alasdair, that no kirk-bells ever rang in Strath Nair. At edge o' dark on Friday, and by the same token the thirteenth day it was, I fell asleep, and dreamed the mools were on my breast, and that the roots of the white daisies were in the hollows where the eyes were that loved you, Alasdair, my son."

The man looked at her with troubled gaze. No words would come. Of what avail to speak when there is nothing to be said? God sends the gloom upon the cloud, and there is rain: God sends the gloom upon the hill, and there is mist: God sends the gloom upon the sun, and there is winter. It is God, too, sends the gloom upon the soul, and there is change. The swallow knows when to lift up her wing over against the shadow that creeps out of the north: the wild swan knows when the smell of snow is behind the sun: the salmon, lone in the [104]brown pool among the hills, hears the deep sea, and his tongue pants for salt, and his fins quiver, and he knows that his time is come, and that the sea calls. The doe knows when the fawn hath not yet quaked in her belly: is not the violet more deep in the shadowy dewy eyes? The woman knows when the babe hath not yet stirred a little hand: is not the wild-rose on her cheek more often seen, and are not the shy tears moist on quiet hands in the dusk? How, then, shall the soul not know when the change is nigh at last? Is it a less thing than a reed, which sees the yellow birch-gold adrift on the lake, and the gown of the heather grow russet when the purple has passed into the sky, and the white bog-down wave gray and tattered where the loneroid grows dark and pungent—which sees, and knows that the breath of the Death-Weaver at the Pole is fast faring along the frozen norland peaks? It is more than a reed, it is more than a wild doe on the hills, it is more than a swallow lifting her wing against the coming of the shadow, it is more than a swan drunken with the savour of the blue wine of the waves when the green [105]Arctic lawns are white and still. It is more than these, which has the Son of God for brother, and is clothed with light. God doth not extinguish at the dark tomb what he hath litten in the dark womb.

Who shall say that the soul knows not when the bird is aweary of the nest, and the nest is aweary of the wind? Who shall say that all portents are vain imaginings? A whirling straw upon the road is but a whirling straw; yet the wind is upon the cheek almost ere it is gone.

It was not for Alasdair Òg, then, to put a word upon the saying of the woman that was his mother, and was age-white, and could see with the seeing of old wise eyes.

So all that was upon his lips was a sigh, and the poor prayer that is only a breath out of the heart.

"You will be telling me, gray sweetheart," he said lovingly, at last—"you will be telling me what was behind the word that you said: that about the foxes that have holes for the hiding, poor beasts, and the birdeens wi' their nests, though the Son o' Man hath not where to lay his head?"

[106]"Ay, Alasdair, my son that I bore long syne an' that I'm leaving soon, I will be for telling you that thing, an' now too, for I am knowing what is in the dark this night o' the nights."

Old Sine put her head back wearily on the chair, and let her hands lie, long and white, palm-downward upon her knees. The peat-glow warmed the dull gray that lurked under her closed eyes and about her mouth, and in the furrowed cheeks. Alasdair moved nearer, and took her right hand in his, where it lay like a tired sheep between two scarped rocks. Gently he smoothed her hand, and wondered why so frail and slight a creature as this small old wizened woman could have mothered a great swarthy man like himself—he a man, now, with his two score and ten years, and yet but a boy there at the dear side of her.

"It was this way, Alasdair-mochree," she went on in her low thin voice,—like a wind-worn leaf, the man that was her son thought. "It was this way. I went down to the burn to wash the *claar*, and when I was there I saw a wounded fawn in the bracken. The [107]big sad eyes of it were like those of Maisie, poor lass, when she had the birthing that was her going-call. I went through the bracken, and down by the Gorromalt, and into the Shadowy Glen.

"And when I was there, and standing by the running water, I saw a man by the stream-side. He was tall, but spare and weary: and the clothes upon him were poor and worn. He had sorrow. When he lifted his head at me, I saw the tears. Dark, wonderful, sweet eyes they were. His face was pale. It was not the face of a man of the hills. There was no red in it, and the eyes looked in upon themselves. He was a fair man, with the white hands that a woman has, a woman like the Bantighearna of Glenchaisteal over yonder. His voice, too, was a voice like that: in the softness, and the sweet, quiet sorrow, I am meaning.

"The word that I gave him was in the English: for I thought he was like a man out of Sasunn, or of the southlands somewhere. But he answered me in the Gaelic: sweet, good Gaelic like that of the Bioball over there, to Himself be the praise.

[108]"'And is it the way down the Strath you are seeking?' I asked: 'and will you not be coming up to the house yonder, poor cot though it is, and have a sup of milk, and a rest if it's weary you are?'

"'You are having my thanks for that,' he said, 'and it is as though I had both the good rest and the cool sweet drink. But I am following the flowing water here.'

"'Is it for the fishing?' I asked.

"'I am a Fisher,' he said, and the voice of him was low and sad. He had no hat on his head, and the light that streamed through a rowan-tree was in his long hair. He had the pity of the poor in his sorrowful gray eyes.

"'And will you not sleep with us?' I asked again: 'that is, if you have no place to go to, and are a stranger in this country, as I am thinking you are; for I have never had sight of you in the home-straths before.'

"'I am a stranger,' he said, 'and I have no home, and my father's house is a great way off.'

"'Do not tell me, poor man,' I said gently, for fear of the pain, 'do not tell me if you [109]would fain not; but it is glad I will be if you will give me the name you have.'

"'My name is Mac-an-t'-Saoir,' he answered with the quiet deep gaze that was his. And with that he bowed his head, and went on his way, brooding deep.

"Well, it was with a heavy heart I turned, and went back through the bracken. A heavy heart, for sure, and yet, oh peace too, cool dews of peace. And the fawn was there: healed, Alasdair, healed, and whinny-bleating for its doe, that stood on a rock wi' lifted hoof an' stared down the glen to where the Fisher was.

"When I was at the burnside, a woman came down the brae. She was fair to see, but the tears were upon her.

"'Oh,' she cried, 'have you seen a man going this way?'

"'Ay, for sure,' I answered, 'but what man would he be?'

"'He is called Mac-an-t'-Saoir.'

"'Well, there are many men that are called Son of the Carpenter. What will his own name be?'

"'Iosa,' she said.

[110]"And when I looked at her, she was weaving the wavy branches of a thorn near by, and sobbing low, and it was like a wreath or crown that she made.

"'And who will you be, poor woman?' I asked.

"'O my Son, my Son,' she said, and put her apron over her head and went down into the Shadowy Glen, she weeping sore, too, at that, poor woman.

"So now, Alasdair, my son, tell me what thought you have about this thing that I have told you. For I know well whom I met on the brae there, and who the Fisher was. And when I was at the peats here once more I sat down, and my mind sank into myself. And it is knowing the knowledge I am."

"Well, well, dear, it is sore tired you are. Have rest now. But sure there are many men called Macintyre."

"Ay, and what Gael that you know will be for giving you his surname like that?"

Alasdair had no word for that. He rose to put some more peats on the fire. When he had done this, he gave a cry.

[111]The whiteness that was on the mother's hair was now in the face. There was no blood there, or in the drawn lips. The light in the old, dim eyes was like water after frost.

He took her hand in his. Clay-cold it was. He let it go, and it fell straight by the chair, stiff as the cromak he carried when he was with the sheep.

"O my God and my God," he whispered, white with the awe, and the bitter cruel pain.

Then it was that he heard a knocking at the door.

"Who is there?" he cried hoarsely.

"Open, and let me in." It was a low, sweet voice; but was that gray hour the time for a welcome?

"Go, but go in peace, whoever you are. There is death here."

"Open, and let me in."

At that, Alasdair, shaking like a reed in the wind, unclasped the latch. A tall, fair man, ill-clad and weary, pale, too, and with dreaming eyes, came in.

"*Beannachd Dhe an Tigh*," he said; "God's blessing on this house, and on all here."

[112]"The same upon yourself," Alasdair said, with a weary pain in his voice. "And who will you be? and forgive the asking."

"I am called Mac-an-t'-Saoir, and Iosa is the name I bear—Jesus, the Son of the Carpenter."

"It is a good name. And is it good you are seeking this night?"

"I am a Fisher."

"Well, that's here an' that's there. But will you go to the Strath over the hill, and tell the good man that is there, the minister, Lachlan MacLachlan, that old Sine nic Leòid, wife of Alasdair Ruadh, is dead."

"I know that, Alasdair Òg."

"And how will you be knowing that, and my name, too, you that are called Macintyre?"

"I met the white soul of Sine as it went down by the Shadowy Glen a brief while ago. She was singing a glad song, she was. She had green youth in her eyes. And a man was holding her by the hand. It was Alasdair Ruadh."

At that Alasdair fell on his knees. When he looked up, there was no one there. [113]Through the darkness outside the door, he saw a star shining white, and leaping like a pulse.

It was three days after that day of shadow that Sine Macleod was put under the green turf.

On each night, Alasdair Òg walked in the Shadowy Glen, and there he saw a man fishing, though ever afar off. Stooping he was, always, and like a shadow at times. But he was the man that was called Iosa Mac-an-t'-Saoir—Jesus, the Son of the Carpenter.

And on the night of the earthing he saw the Fisher close by.

"Lord God," he said, with the hush on his voice, and deep awe in his wondering eyes: "Lord God!"

And the Man looked at him.

"Night and day, Alasdair MacAlasdair," he said, "night and day I fish in the waters of the world. And these waters are the waters of grief, and the waters of sorrow, and the waters of despair. And it is the souls of the living I fish for. And lo, I say this thing unto you, for you shall not see me again: *Go in peace.* Go in peace, good soul of a poor man, for thou hast seen the Fisher of Men."

[117]

THE LAST SUPPER

> "... and there shall beBeautiful things made new...."
>
> Hyperion.

THE last time that the Fisher of Men was seen in Strath Nair was not of Alasdair Macleod but of the little child, Art Macarthur, him that was born of the woman Mary Gilchrist, that had known the sorrow of women.

He was a little child, indeed, when, because of his loneliness and having lost his way, he lay sobbing among the bracken by the stream-side in the Shadowy Glen.

When he was a man, and had reached the gloaming of his years, he was loved of men and women, for his songs are many and sweet, and his heart was true, and he was a good man and had no evil against any one.

It is he who saw the Fisher of Men, when he was but a little lad; and some say that it was on the eve of the day that Alasdair Òg died, though of this I know nothing. And what he saw, and what he heard, was a moonbeam [118]that fell into the dark sea of his mind, and sank therein, and filled it with light for all the days of his life. A moonlit mind was that of Art Macarthur: him that is known best as Ian Mòr, Ian Mòr of the Hills, though why he took the name of Ian Cameron is known to none now but one person, and that need not be for the telling here. He had music always in his mind. I asked him once why he heard what so few heard, but he smiled and said only: "When the heart is full of love, cool dews of peace rise from it and fall upon the mind: and that is when the song of Joy is heard." It must have been because of this shining of his soul that some who loved him thought of him as one illumined. His mind was a shell that held the haunting echo of the deep seas: and to know him was to catch a breath of the infinite ocean of wonder and mystery and beauty of which he was the quiet oracle. He has peace now, where he lies under the heather upon a hillside far away: but the Fisher of Men will send him hitherward again, to put a light upon the wave, and a gleam upon the brown earth.

[119]I will tell this *sgeul* as Ian Mòr, that was the little child Art Macarthur, told it to me.

Often and often it is to me all as a dream that comes unawares. Often and often have I striven to see into the green glens of the mind whence it comes, and whither, in a flash, in a rainbow gleam, it vanishes. When I seek to draw close to it, to know whether it is a winged glory out of the soul, or was indeed a thing that happened to me in my tender years, lo—it is a dawn drowned in day, a star lost in the sun, the falling of dew.

But I will not be forgetting: no, never; no, not till the silence of the grass is over my eyes: I will not be forgetting that gloaming.

Bitter tears are those that children have. All that we say with vain words is said by them in this welling spray of pain. I had the sorrow that day. Strange hostilities lurked in the familiar bracken. The soughing of the wind among the trees, the wash of the brown water by my side, that had been companionable, were voices of awe. The quiet light upon the grass flamed.

The fierce people that lurked in shadow had [120]eyes for my helplessness. When the dark came I thought I should be dead, devoured of I knew not what wild creature. Would mother never come, never come with saving arms, with eyes like soft candles of home?

Then my sobs grew still, for I heard a step. With dread upon me, poor wee lad that I was, I looked to see who came out of the wilderness. It was a man, tall and thin and worn, with long hair hanging adown his face. Pale he was as a moonlit cot on the dark moor, and his voice was low and sweet. When I saw his eyes, I had no fear upon me at all. I saw the mother-look in the gray shadow of them.

"And is that you, Art lennavan-mo?" he said, as he stooped and lifted me.

I had no fear. The wet was out of my eyes.

"What is it you will be listening to, now, my little lad?" he whispered, as he saw me lean, intent, to catch I know not what.

"Sure," I said, "I am not for knowing; but I thought I heard a music away down there in the wood."

I heard it, for sure. It was a wondrous sweet air, as of one playing the feadan in a dream. [121]Callum Dall, the piper, could give no rarer music than that was; and Callum was a seventh son, and was born in the moonshine.

"Will you come with me this night of the nights, little Art?" the man asked me, with his lips touching my brow and giving me rest.

"That I will indeed and indeed," I said. And then I fell asleep.

When I woke we were in the huntsman's booth that is at the far end of the Shadowy Glen.

There was a long rough-hewn table in it, and I stared when I saw bowls and a great jug of milk and a plate heaped with oatcakes, and beside it a brown loaf of rye-bread.

"Little Art," said he who carried me, "are you for knowing now who I am?"

"You are a prince, I'm thinking," was the shy word that came to my mouth.

"Sure, lennav-aghray, that is so. It is called the Prince of Peace I am."

"And who is to be eating all this?" I asked.

"This is the last supper," the prince said, so low that I could scarce hear; and it [122]seemed to me that he whispered, "for I die daily, and ever ere I die the Twelve break bread with me."

It was then I saw that there were six bowls of porridge on the one side and six on the other.

"What is your name, O Prince?"

"Iosa."

"And will you have no other name than that?"

"I am called Iosa mac Dhe."

"And is it living in this house you are?"

"Ay. But Art, my little lad, I will kiss your eyes, and you shall see who sup with me."

And with that the prince that was called Iosa kissed me on the eyes, and I saw.

"You will never be quite blind again," he whispered, and that is why all the long years of my years I have been glad in my soul.

What I saw was a thing strange and wonderful. Twelve men sat at that table, and all had eyes of love upon Iosa. But they were not like any men I had ever seen. Tall and fair and terrible they were, like morning [123]in a desert place; all save one, who was dark, and had a shadow upon him and in his wild eyes.

It seemed to me that each was clad in radiant mist. The eyes of them were as stars through that mist.

And each, before he broke bread, or put spoon to the porridge that was in the bowl before him, laid down upon the table three shuttles. Long I looked upon that company, but Iosa held me in his arms, and I had no fear.

"Who are these men?" he asked me.

"The Sons of God," I said; I not knowing what I said, for it was but a child I was.

He smiled at that. "Behold," he spoke to the twelve men who sat at the table, "behold the little one is wiser than the wisest of ye." At that all smiled with the gladness and the joy, save one: him that was in the shadow. He looked at me, and I remembered two black lonely tarns upon the hillside, black with the terror because of the kelpie and the drowner.

"Who are these men?" I whispered, with [124]the tremor on me, that was come of the awe I had.

"They are the Twelve Weavers, Art, my little child."

"And what is their weaving?"

"They weave for my Father, whose web I am."

At that I looked upon the prince, but I could see no web.

"Are you not Iosa the Prince?"

"I am the Web of Life, Art lennavan-mo."

"And what are the three shuttles that are beside each Weaver?"

I know now that when I turned my child's eyes upon these shuttles I saw that they were alive and wonderful, and never the same to the seeing.

"They are called *Beauty* and *Wonder* and *Mystery*."

And with that Iosa mac Dhe sat down and talked with the Twelve. All were passing fair, save him who looked sidelong out of dark eyes. I thought each, as I looked at him, more beautiful than any of his fellows; but most I loved to look at the twain who sat on either side of Iosa.

[125]"He will be a Dreamer among men," said the prince; "so tell him who ye are."

Then he who was on the right turned his eyes upon me. I leaned to him, laughing low with the glad pleasure I had because of his eyes and shining hair, and the flame as of the blue sky that was his robe.

"I am the Weaver of Joy," he said. And with that he took his three shuttles that were called Beauty and Wonder and Mystery, and he wove an immortal shape, and it went forth of the room and out into the green world, singing a rapturous sweet song.

Then he that was upon the left of Iosa the Life, looked at me, and my heart leaped. He, too, had shining hair, but I could not tell the colour of his eyes for the glory that was in them. "I am the Weaver of Love," he said; "and I sit next the heart of Iosa." And with that he took his three shuttles that were called Beauty and Wonder and Mystery, and he wove an immortal shape, and it went forth of the room and out into the green world, singing a rapturous sweet song.

Even then, child as I was, I wished to [126]look on no other. None could be so passing fair, I thought, as the Weaver of Joy and the Weaver of Love.

But a wondrous sweet voice sang in my ears, and a cool, soft hand laid itself upon my head, and the beautiful lordly one who had spoken said, "I am the Weaver of Death," and the lovely whispering one who had lulled me with rest said, "I am the Weaver of Sleep." And each wove with the shuttles of Beauty and Wonder and Mystery, and I knew not which was the more fair, and Death seemed to me as Love, and in the eyes of Dream I saw Joy.

My gaze was still upon the fair wonderful shapes that went forth from these twain,—from the Weaver of Sleep, an immortal shape of star-eyed Silence, and from the Weaver of Death a lovely Dusk with a heart of hidden flame—when I heard the voice of two others of the Twelve. They were like the laughter of the wind in the corn, and like the golden fire upon that corn. And the one said, "I am the Weaver of Passion," and when he spoke I thought that he was both Love and Joy, and Death and Life, and I put out my [127]hands. "It is Strength I give," he said; and he took and kissed me. Then, while Iosa took me again upon his knee, I saw the Weaver of Passion turn to the white glory beside him,—him that Iosa whispered to me was the secret of the world, and that was called "The Weaver of Youth." I know not whence nor how it came, but there was a singing of skyey birds when these twain took the shuttles of Beauty and Wonder and Mystery and wove each an immortal shape, and bade it go forth out of the room into the green world, to sing there for ever and ever in the ears of man a rapturous sweet song.

"O Iosa," I cried, "are these all thy brethren? for each is fair as thee, and all have lit their eyes at the white fire I see now in thy heart."

But, before he spake, the room was filled with music. I trembled with the joy, and in my ears it has lingered ever, nor shall ever go. Then I saw that it was the breathing of the seventh and eighth, of the ninth and the tenth of those star-eyed ministers of Iosa whom he called the Twelve: and the names of them were the Weaver of Laughter, the [128]Weaver of Tears, the Weaver of Prayer, and the Weaver of Peace. Each rose and kissed me there. "We shall be with you to the end, little Art," they said: and I took hold of the hand of one, and cried, "O beautiful one, be likewise with the woman my mother," and there came back to me the whisper of the Weaver of Tears: "I will, unto the end."

Then, wonderingly, I watched him likewise take the shuttles that were ever the same and yet never the same, and weave an immortal shape. And when this soul of Tears went forth of the room, I thought it was my mother's voice singing that rapturous sweet song, and I cried out to it.

The fair immortal turned and waved to me. "I shall never be far from thee, little Art," it sighed, like summer rain falling on leaves: "but I go now to my home in the heart of women."

There were now but two out of the Twelve. Oh the gladness and the joy when I looked at him who had his eyes fixed on the face of Iosa that was the Life! He lifted the three shuttles of Beauty and Wonder and Mystery, and he wove a Mist of Rainbows in that [129]room; and in the glory I saw that even the dark twelfth one lifted up his eyes and smiled.

"O what will the name of you be!" I cried, straining my arms to the beautiful lordly one. But he did not hear, for he wrought Rainbow after Rainbow out of the mist of glory that he made, and sent each out into the green world, to be for ever before the eyes of men.

"He is the Weaver of Hope," whispered Iosa mac Dhe, "and he is the soul of each that is here."

Then I turned to the twelfth, and said, "Who art thou, O lordly one with the shadow in the eyes?"

But he answered not, and there was silence in the room. And all there, from the Weaver of Joy to the Weaver of Peace, looked down, and said nought. Only the Weaver of Hope wrought a rainbow, and it drifted into the heart of the lonely Weaver that was twelfth.

"And who will this man be, O Iosa mac Dhe?" I whispered.

"Answer the little child," said Iosa, and his voice was sad.

[130]Then the Weaver answered.

"I am the Weaver of Glory"—he began, but Iosa looked at him, and he said no more.

"Art, little lad," said the Prince of Peace, "he is the one who betrayeth me for ever. He is Judas, the Weaver of Fear."

And at that the sorrowful shadow-eyed man that was the twelfth took up the three shuttles that were before him.

"And what are these, O Judas?" I cried eagerly, for I saw that they were black.

When he answered not one of the Twelve leaned forward and looked at him. It was the Weaver of Death who did this thing.

"The three shuttles of Judas the Fear-Weaver, O little Art," said the Weaver of Death, "are called Mystery, and Despair, and the Grave."

And with that Judas rose and left the room. But the shape that he had woven went forth with him as his shadow: and each fared out into the dim world, and the Shadow entered into the minds and into the hearts of men, and betrayed Iosa that was the Prince of Peace.

[131]Thereupon, Iosa rose, and took me by the hand and led me out of that room. When, once, I looked back I saw none of the Twelve save only the Weaver of Hope, and he sat singing a wild sweet song that he had learned of the Weaver of Joy, sat singing amid a mist of rainbows and weaving a radiant glory that was dazzling as the sun.

And at that I woke, and was against my mother's heart, and she with the tears upon me, and her lips moving in a prayer.

[135]

THE DARK NAMELESS ONE

ONE day this summer I sailed with Padruic Macrae and Ivor McLean,

boatmen of Iona, along the southwestern reach of the Ross of Mull.

The whole coast of the Ross is indescribably wild and desolate. From Feenafort (Fhionn-phort) opposite Balliemore of Icolmkill, to the hamlet of Earraid Lighthouse, it were hardly exaggeration to say that the whole tract is uninhabited by man and unenlivened by any green thing. It is the haunt of the cormorant and the seal.

No one who has not visited this region can realise its barrenness. Its one beauty is the faint bloom which lies upon it in the sunlight—a bloom which becomes as the glow of an inner flame when the sun westers without cloud or mist. This is from the ruddy hue of the granite, of which all that wilderness is wrought.

[136]It is a land tortured by the sea, scourged by the sea-wind. A myriad lochs, fiords, inlets, passages, serrate its broken frontiers. Innumerable islets and reefs, fanged like ravenous wolves, sentinel every shallow, lurk in every strait. He must be a skilled boatman who would take the Sound of Earraid and penetrate the reaches of the Ross.

There are many days in the months of peace, as the islanders call the period from Easter till the autumnal equinox, when Earraid and the rest of Ross seem under a spell. It is the spell of beauty. Then the yellow light of the sun is upon the tumbled masses and precipitous shelves and ledges, ruddy petals or leaves of that vast Flower of Granite. Across it the cloud shadows trail their purple elongations, their scythe-sweep curves, and abrupt evanishing floodings of warm dusk. From wet boulder to boulder, from crag to shelly crag, from fissure to fissure, the sea ceaselessly weaves a girdle of foam. When the wide luminous stretch of waters beyond—green near the land, and farther out all of a living blue, interspersed with wide alleys of amethyst—is white with the [137]sea-horses, there is such a laughter of surge and splash all the way from Slugan-dubh to the Rudha-nam-Maol-Mòra, or to the tide-swept promontory of the Sgeireig-a'-Bhochdaidh, that, looking inland, one sees through a rainbow-shimmering veil of ever-flying spray.

But the sun spell is even more fugitive upon the face of this wild land than the spell of beauty upon a woman. So runs one of our proverbs: as the falling of the wave, as the fading of the leaf, so is the beauty of a woman, unless—ah, that *unless*, and the indiscoverable fount of joy that can only be come upon by hazard once in life, and thereafter only in dreams, and the Land of the Rainbow that is never reached, and the green sea-doors of Tir-na-thonn, that open now no more to any wandering wave!

It was from Ivor McLean, on that day, I heard the strange tale of his kinsman Murdoch, the tale of "The Ninth Wave" that I have told elsewhere. It was Padruic, however, who told me of the Sea-witch of Earraid.

"Yes," he said, "I have heard of the [138]*uisge-each*" (the sea-beast, sea-kelpie, or water-horse), "but I have never seen it with the eyes. My father and my brother knew of it. But this thing I know, and this what we call *an-cailleach-uisge*" (the siren or water-witch); "the *cailliach*, mind you, not the *maighdeann-mhàra*" (the mermaid), "who means no harm. May she hear my saying it! The cailliach is old and clad in weeds, but her voice is young, and she always sits so that the light is in the eyes of the beholder. She seems to him young also, and fair. She has two familiars in the form of seals, one black as the grave, and the other white as the shroud that is in the grave; and these sometimes upset a boat, if the sailor laughs at the uisge-cailliach's song.

"A man netted one of those seals, more than a hundred years ago, with his herring-trawl, and dragged it into the boat; but the other seal tore at the net so savagely, with its head and paws over the bows, that it was clear no net would long avail. The man heard them crying and screaming, and then talking low and muttering, like women in [139]a frenzy. In his fear he cast the nets adrift, all but a small portion that was caught in the thwarts. Afterwards, in this portion, he found a tress of woman's hair. And that is just so: to the Stones be it said.

"The grandson of this man, Tomais McNair, is still living, a shepherd on Eilean-Uamhain, beyond Lunga in the Cairnburg Isles. A few years ago, off Callachan Point, he saw the two seals, and heard, though he did not see, the cailliach. And that which I tell you,—Christ's Cross before me—is a true thing."

All the time that Padruic was speaking I saw that Ivor McLean looked away: either as though he heard nothing, or did not wish to hear. There was dream in his eyes; I saw that, so said nothing for a time.

"What is it, Ivor?" I asked at last, in a low voice. He started, and looked at me strangely.

"What will you be asking that for? What are you doing in my mind, that is secret?"

"I see that you are brooding over something. Will you not tell me?"

"Tell her," said Padruic quietly.

[140]But Ivor kept silent. There was a look in his eyes which I understood. Thereafter we sailed on, with no word in the boat at all.

That night, a dark, rainy night it was, with an uplift wind beating high over against the hidden moon, I went to the cottage where Ivor McLean lived with his old deaf mother,—deaf nigh upon twenty years, ever since the night of the nights when she heard the women whisper that Callum, her husband, was among the drowned, after a death-wind had blown.

When I entered, he was sitting before the flaming coal-fire; for on Iona, now, by decree of MacCailin Mòr, there is no more peat burned.

"You will tell me now, Ivor?" was all I said.

"Yes; I will be telling you now. And the reason why I did not tell you before was because it is not a wise or a good thing to tell ancient stories about the sea while still on the running wave. Macrae should not have done that thing. It may be we shall suffer for it when next we go out with the nets. We were to go to-night: but no, not I, no, [141]no, for sure, not for all the herring in the Sound."

"Is it an ancient *sgeul*, Ivor?"

"Ay. I am not for knowing the age of these things. It may be as old as the days of the Féinn for all I know. It has come down to us. Alasdair MacAlasdair of Tiree, him that used to boast of having all the stories of Colum and Brighde, it was he told it to the mother of my mother, and she to me."

"What is it called?"

"Well, this and that; but there is no harm in saying it is called the Dark Nameless One."

"The Dark Nameless One!"

"It is this way. But will you ever have been hearing of the MacOdrums of Uist?"

"Ay: the Sliochd-nan-ròn."

"That is so. God knows. The Sliochd-nan-ròn ... the progeny of the Seal.... Well, well, no man knows what moves in the shadow of life. And now I will be telling you that old ancient tale, as it was given to me by the mother of my mother."

[142]On a day of the days, Colum was walking alone by the sea-shore. The monks were at the hoe or the spade, and some milking the kye, and some at the fishing. They say it was on the first day of the *Faoilleach Geamhraidh*, the day that is called *Am fheill Brighde*.

The holy man had wandered on to where the rocks are, opposite to Soa. He was praying and praying, and it is said that whenever he prayed aloud, the barren egg in the nest would quicken, and the blighted bud unfold, and the butterfly cleave its shroud.

Of a sudden he came upon a great black seal, lying silent on the rocks, with wicked eyes.

"My blessing upon you, O Ròn," he said with the good kind courteousness that was his.

"*Droch spadadh ort*," answered the seal. "A bad end to you, Colum of the Gown."

"Sure, now," said Colum angrily, "I am knowing by that curse that you are no friend of Christ, but of the evil pagan faith out of the north. For here I am known ever as Colum [143]the White, or as Colum the Saint: and it is only the Picts and the wanton Normen who deride me because of the holy white robe I wear."

"Well, well," replied the seal, speaking the good Gaelic as though it were the tongue of the deep sea, as God knows it may be for all you, I, or the blind wind can say: "Well, well, let that thing be: it's a wave-way here or a wave-way there. But now if it is a Druid you are, whether of Fire or of Christ, be telling me where my woman is, and where my little daughter."

At this, Colum looked at him for a long while. Then he knew.

"It is a man you were once, O Ròn?"

"Maybe ay and maybe no."

"And with that thick Gaelic that you have, it will be out of the north Isles you come?"

"That is a true thing."

"Now I am for knowing at last who and what you are. You are one of the race of Odrum the Pagan."

"Well, I am not denying it, Colum. And what is more, I am Angus MacOdrum, [144]Aonghas mac Torcall mhic Odrum, and the name I am known by is Black Angus."

"A fitting name too," said Colum the Holy, "because of the black sin in your heart, and the black end God has in store for you."

At that Black Angus laughed.

"Why is there laughter upon you, Man-Seal?"

"Well, it is because of the good company I'll be having. But, now, give me the word: are you for having seen or heard aught of a woman called Kirsteen McVurich?"

"Kirsteen—Kirsteen—that is the good name of a nun it is, and no sea-wanton!"

"Oh, a name here or a name there is soft sand. And so you cannot be for telling me where my woman is?"

"No."

"Then a stake for your belly, and the nails through your hands, thirst on your tongue, and the corbies at your eyne!"

And, with that, Black Angus louped into the green water, and the hoarse wild laugh of him sprang into the air and fell dead against the cliff like a wind-spent mew.

[145]Colum went slowly back to the brethren, brooding deep. "God is good," he said in a low voice, again and again; and each time that he spoke there came a fair sweet daisy into the grass, or a yellow bird rose up, with song to it for the first time, wonderful and sweet to hear.

As he drew near to the House of God, he met Murtagh, an old monk of the ancient old race of the isles.

"Who is Kirsteen McVurich, Murtagh?" he asked.

"She was a good servant of Christ, she was, in the south isles, O Colum, till Black Angus won her to the sea."

"And when was that?"

"Nigh upon a thousand years ago."

At that, Colum stared in amaze. But Murtagh was a man of truth, nor did he speak in allegories. "Ay, Colum my father, nigh upon a thousand years ago."

"But can mortal sin live as long as that?"

"Ay, it endureth. Long, long ago, before Oisìn sang, before Fionn, before Cuchullin was a glorious great prince, and in the days when the Tuatha De Danann were sole lords in all green Banba, Black Angus made the woman Kirsteen McVurich leave the place of prayer and go down to the sea-shore, and there he leaped upon her, and made her his prey, and she followed him into the sea."

"And is death above her now?"

"No. She is the woman that weaves the sea-spells at the wild place out yonder that is known as Earraid: she that is called *an-Cailleach-uisge*, the sea-witch."

"Then why was Black Angus for the seeking her here and the seeking her there?"

"It is the Doom. It is Adam's first wife she is, that sea-witch over there, where the foam is ever in the sharp fangs of the rocks."

"And who will he be?"

"His body is the body of Angus the son of Torcall of the race of Odrum, for all that a seal he is to the seeming; but the soul of him is Judas."

"Black Judas, Murtagh?"

"Ay, Black Judas, Colum."

But with that, Ivor McLean rose abruptly from before the fire, saying that he would speak no more that night. And truly enough there was a wild, lone, desolate cry in the wind, and a slapping of the waves one upon the other with an eerie laughing sound, and the screaming of a sea-mew that was like a human thing.

So I touched the shawl of his mother, who looked up with startled eyes and said, "God be with us;" and then I opened the door, and the salt smell of the wrack was in my nostrils, and the great drowning blackness of the night.

THE THREE MARVELS OF HY

[150]

I. THE FESTIVAL OF THE BIRDS.

II. THE SABBATH OF THE FISHES AND THE FLIES.

III. THE MOON-CHILD.

[151]

I

THE FESTIVAL OF THE BIRDS

BEFORE dawn, on the morning of the hundredth Sabbath after Colum the White had made glory to God in Hy, that was theretofore called Ioua and thereafter I-shona and is now Iona, the Saint beheld his own Sleep in a vision.

Much fasting and long pondering over the missals, with their golden and azure and sea-green initials and earth-brown branching letters, had made Colum weary. He had brooded much of late upon the mystery of the living world that was not man's world.

On the eve of that hundredth Sabbath, which was to be a holy festival in Iona, he had talked long with an ancient graybeard out of a remote isle in the north, the wild Isle of the Mountains where Scathach the [152]Queen hanged the men of Lochlin by their yellow hair.

This man's name was Ardan, and he was of the ancient people. He had come to Hy because of two things. Maolmòr, the King of the northern Picts, had sent him to learn of Colum what was this god-teaching he had brought out of Eiré: and for himself he had come, with his age upon him, to see what manner of man this Colum was, who had made Ioua, that was "Innis-nan-Dhruidhneach"—the Isle of the Druids—into a place of new worship.

For three hours Ardan and Colum had walked by the sea-shore. Each learned of the other. Ardan bowed his head before the wisdom. Colum knew in his heart that the Druid saw mysteries. In the first hour they talked of God. Colum spake, and Ardan smiled in his shadowy eyes. "It is for the knowing," he said, when Colum ceased.

"Ay, sure," said the Saint: "and now, O Ardan the wise, is my God thy God?"

But at that Ardan smiled not. He turned the grave, sad eyes of him to the west. With his right hand he pointed to the Sun that [153]was like a great golden flower. "Truly, He is thy God and my God." Colum was silent. Then he said: "Thee and thine, O Ardan, from Maolmòr the Pictish king to the least of thy slaves, shall have a long weariness in Hell. That fiery globe yonder is but the Lamp of the World: and sad is the case of the man who knows not the torch from the torch-bearer."

And in the second hour they talked of Man. Ardan spake, and Colum smiled in his deep, gray eyes.

"It is for laughter that," he said, when Ardan ceased.

"And why will that be, O Colum of Eiré?" said Ardan. Then the smile went out of Colum's gray eyes, and he turned and looked about him.

He beheld, near, a crow, a horse, and a hound.

"These are thy brethren," he said scornfully.

But Ardan answered quietly, "Even so."

The third hour they talked about the beasts of the earth and the fowls of the air.

At the last Ardan said: "The ancient wisdom hath it that these are the souls of men and women, that have been, or are to be."

[154]Whereat Colum answered: "The new wisdom, that is old as eternity, declareth that God created all things in love. Therefore are we at one, O Ardan, though we sail to the Isle of Truth from the West and the East. Let there be peace between us."

"Peace," said Ardan.

That eve, Ardan of the Picts sat with the monks of Iona. Colum blessed him and said a saying. Oran of the Songs sang a hymn of beauty. Ardan rose, and put the wine of guests to his lips, and chanted this rune:

> O Colum and monks of Christ,It is peace we are having this night:Sure, peace is a good thing,And I am glad with the gladness.
>> We worship one God,Though ye call him Dè—And I say not, *O Dia!*But cry *Bea'uil!*
>> For it is one faith for man,And one for the living world,And no man is wiser than another—And none knoweth much.
>> None knoweth a better thing than this:The Sword, Love, Song, Honour, Sleep.None knoweth a surer thing than this:Birth, Sorrow, Pain, Weariness, Death.
>> [155]Sure, peace is a good thing;Let us be glad of Peace:We are not men of the Sword,But of the Rune and the Wisdom.
>> I have learned a truth of Colum,He hath learned of me:All ye on the morrow shall seeA wonder of the wonders.
>> The thought is on you, that the CrossIs known only of you:Lo, I tell you the birds know itThat are marked with the Sorrow.
>> Listen to the Birds of Sorrow,They shall tell you a great Joy:It is Peace you will be having,With the Birds.

No more would Ardan say after that, though all besought him.

Many pondered long that night. Oran made a song of mystery. Colum brooded through the dark; but before dawn he slept upon the fern that strewed his cell. At dawn, with waking eyes, and weary, he saw his Sleep in a vision.

It stood gray and wan beside him.

"What art thou, O Spirit?" he said.

[156]"I am thy Sleep, Colum."

"And is it peace?"

"It is peace."

"What wouldest thou?"

"I have wisdom. Thy heart and thy brain were closed. I could not give you what I brought. I brought wisdom."

"Give it."

"Behold!"

And Colum, sitting upon the strewed fern that was his bed, rubbed his eyes that were heavy with weariness and fasting and long prayer. He could not see his Sleep now. It was gone, as smoke that is licked up by the wind.

But on the ledge of the hole that was in the eastern wall of his cell he saw a bird. He leaned his elbow upon the leabhar-aifrionn that was by his side. [3] Then he spoke.

> [3] The "leabhar-aifrionn" (pron. lyo-ur-eff-runn) is a missal: literally a mass-book, or chapel-book. Bru-dhearg is literally red-breast.

"Is there song upon thee, O Bru-dhearg?"

Then the Redbreast sang, and the singing was so sweet that tears came into the eyes of Colum, and he thought the sunlight that was [157]streaming from the east was melted into that lilting sweet song. It was a hymn that the Bru-dhearg sang, and it was this:

> Holy, Holy, Holy,Christ upon the Cross;My little nest was near,Hidden in the moss.
> > Holy, Holy, Holy,Christ was pale and wan:His eyes beheld me singing*Bron, Bron, mo Bron*![4]

Holy, Holy, Holy,"Come near, O wee brown bird!"Christ spake: and low I lightedUpon the Living World.

Holy, Holy, Holy,I heard the mocking scorn!But *Holy, Holy, Holy*,I sang against a thorn!

Holy, Holy, Holy,Ah, his brow was bloody;Holy, Holy, Holy,All my breast was ruddy.

Holy, Holy, Holy,Christ's-Bird shalt thou be:Thus said Mary VirginThere on Calvary.

[158]Holy, Holy, Holy,A wee brown bird am I:But my breast is ruddyFor I saw Christ die.

Holy, Holy, Holy,By this ruddy feather,Colum, call thy monks, andAll the birds together.

[4] "O my Grief, my Grief!"

And at that Colum rose. Awe was upon him, and joy.

He went out, and told all to the monks. Then he said Mass out on the green sward. The yellow sunshine was warm upon his gray hair. The love of God was warm in his heart.

"Come, all ye birds!" he cried.

And lo, all the birds of the air flew nigh. The golden eagle soared from the Cuchullins in far-off Skye, and the osprey from the wild lochs of Mull; the gannet from above the clouds, and the fulmar and petrel from the green wave: the cormorant and the skua from the weedy rock, and the plover and the kestrel from the machar: the corbie and the raven from the moor, and the snipe and the bittern and the heron: the cuckoo and cushat [159]from the woodland; the crane from the swamps, the lark from the sky, and the mavis and the merle from the green bushes: the yellowyite, the shilfa, and the lintie, the gyalvonn and the wren and the redbreast, one and all, every creature of the wings, they came at the bidding.

"Peace!" cried Colum.

"Peace!" cried all the Birds, and even the Eagle, the Kestrel, the Corbie, and the Raven cried *Peace, Peace!*

"I will say the Mass," said Colum the White.

And with that he said the Mass. And he blessed the birds. When the last chant was sung, only Bru-dhearg remained.

"Come, O Ruddy-Breast," said Colum, "and sing to us of the Christ."

Through a golden hour thereafter the Redbreast sang. Sweet was the joy of it.

At the end, Colum said "Peace! In the Name of the Father, the Son, and the Holy Ghost."

Thereat Ardan the Pict bowed his head, and in a loud voice repeated—"Sìth (shee)! *An ainm an Athar, 's an mhic, 's an Spioraid Naoimh!*"

And to this day the song of the Birds of Colum, as they are called in Hy, is *Sìth—Sìth—Sìth—an—ainm—Chriosd*—"Peace—Peace—Peace—in the name of Christ!"

II

THE SABBATH OF THE FISHES AND THE FLIES

FOR three days Colum had fasted, save for a mouthful of meal at dawn, a piece of rye-bread at noon, and a mouthful of dulse and spring-water at sundown. On the night of the third day, Oran and Keir came to him in his cell. Colum was on his knees, lost in prayer. There was no sound there, save the faint whispered muttering of his lips, and on the plastered wall the weary buzzing of a fly.

"Master!" said Oran in a low voice, soft with pity and awe, "Master!"

But Colum took no notice. His lips still moved, and the tangled hairs below his nether lip shivered with his failing breath.

"Father!" said Keir, tender as a woman, "Father!"

[162]Colum did not turn his eyes from the wall. The fly droned his drowsy hum upon the rough plaster. It crawled wearily for a space, then stopped. The slow hot drone filled the cell.

"Master," said Oran, "it is the will of the brethren that you break your fast. You are old, and God has your glory. Give us peace."

"Father," urged Keir, seeing that Colum kneeled unnoticingly, his lips still moving above his black beard, with the white hair of him falling about his head like a snowdrift slipping from a boulder. "Father, be pitiful! We hunger and thirst for your presence. We can fast no longer, yet have we no heart to break our fast if you are not with us. Come, holy one, and be of our company, and eat of the good broiled fish that awaiteth us. We perish for the benediction of thine eyes."

Then it was that Colum rose, and walked slowly towards the wall.

"Little black beast," he said to the fly that droned its drowsy hum and moved not at all; "little black beast, sure it is well I [163]am knowing what you are. You are thinking you are going to get my blessing, you that have come out of hell for the soul of me!"

At that the fly flew heavily from the wall, and slowly circled round and round the head of Colum the White.

"What think you of that, brother Oran, brother Keir?" he asked in a low voice, hoarse because of his long fast and the weariness that was upon him.

"It is a fiend," said Oran.

"It is an angel," said Keir.

Thereupon the fly settled upon the wall again, and again droned his drowsy hot hum.

"Little black beast," said Colum, with the frown coming down into his eyes, "is it for peace you are here, or for sin? Answer, I conjure you in the name of the Father, the Son, and the Holy Ghost!"

"*An ainm an Athar, 's an Mhic, 's an Spioraid Naoimh,*" repeated Oran below his breath.

"*An ainm an Athar, 's an Mhic, 's an Spioraid Naoimh,*" repeated Keir below his breath.

Then the fly that was upon the wall flew up to the roof and circled to and fro. And it sang a beautiful song, and its song was this:

I

Praise be to God, and a blessing too at that, and a blessing!For Colum the White, Colum the Dove, hath worshipped;Yea, he hath worshipped and made of a desert a garden,And out of the dung of men's souls hath made a sweet savour of burning.

II

A savour of burning, most sweet, a fire for the altar,This he hath made in the desert; the hell-saved all gladden.Sure he hath put his benison, too, on milch-cow and bullock,On the fowls of the air, and the man-eyed seals, and the otter.

III

But where in his Dûn in the great blue mainland of HeavenGod the All-Father broodeth, where the harpers are harping his glory;There where He sitteth, where a river of ale poureth ever,His great sword broken, His spear in the dust, He broodeth.

IV

And this is the thought that moves in his brain, as a cloud filled with thunderMoves through the vast hollow sky filled with the dust of the stars:*What boots it the glory of Colum, since he maketh a Sabbath to bless me,And hath no thought of my sons in the deeps of the air and the sea?*

And with that the fly passed from their vision. In the cell was a most wondrous sweet song, like the sound of far-off pipes over water.

Oran said in a low voice of awe, "O our God!"

Keir whispered, white with fear, "O God, my God!"

But Colum rose, and took a scourge from where it hung on the wall. "It shall be for peace, Oran," he said, with a grim smile flitting like a bird above the nest of his black beard; "it shall be for peace, Keir!"

And with that he laid the scourge heavily upon the bent backs of Keir and Oran, nor stayed his hand, nor let his three days' fast weaken the deep piety that was in the might of his arm, and because of the glory to God.

Then, when he was weary, peace came into his heart, and he sighed "*Amen!*"

"Amen!" said Oran the monk.

"Amen!" said Keir the monk.

"And this thing hath been done," said Colum, "because of the evil wish of you and the brethren, that I should break my fast, and eat of fish, till God willeth it. And lo, I have learned a mystery. Ye shall all witness to it on the morrow, which is the Sabbath."

That night the monks wondered much. Only Oran and Keir cursed the fishes in the deeps of the sea and the flies in the deeps of the air.

On the morrow, when the sun was yellow on the brown sea-weed, and there was peace on the isle and upon the waters, Colum and the brotherhood went slowly towards the sea.

At the meadows that are close to the sea, the Saint stood still. All bowed their heads.

"O winged things of the air," cried Colum, "draw near!"

With that the air was full of the hum of [167]innumerable flies, midges, bees, wasps, moths, and all winged insects. These settled upon the monks, who moved not, but praised God in silence. "Glory and praise to God," cried Colum, "behold the Sabbath of the children of God that inhabit the deeps of the air! Blessing and peace be upon them."

"Peace! Peace!" cried the monks, with one voice.

"In the name of the Father, the Son, and the Holy Ghost!" cried Colum the White, glad because of the glory to God.

"*An ainm an Athar, 's an Mhic, 's an Spioraid Naoimh*," cried the monks, bowing reverently, and Oran and Keir deepest of all, because they saw the fly that was of Colum's cell leading the whole host, as though it were their captain, and singing to them a marvellous sweet song.

Oran and Keir testified to this thing, and all were full of awe and wonder, and Colum praised God.

Then the Saints and the brotherhood moved onward and went upon the rocks. When all stood ankle-deep in the sea-weed that was swaying in the tide, Colum cried:

[168]"O finny creatures of the deep, draw near!"

And with that the whole sea shimmered as with silver and gold.

All the fishes of the sea, and the great eels, and the lobsters and the crabs, came in a swift and terrible procession. Great was the glory.

Then Colum cried, "O fishes of the Deep, who is your king?"

Whereupon the herring, the mackerel, and the dog-fish swam forward, and each claimed to be king. But the echo that ran from wave to wave said, *The Herring is King*.

Then Colum said to the mackerel: "Sing the song that is upon you!"

And the mackerel sang the song of the wild rovers of the sea, and the lust of pleasure.

Then Colum said, "But for God's mercy, I would curse you, O false fish."

Then he spake likewise to the dog-fish: and the dog-fish sang of slaughter and the chase, and the joy of blood.

And Colum said: "Hell shall be your portion."

And there was peace. And the Herring said:

"In the name of the Father, the Son, and the Holy Ghost!"

Whereat all that mighty multitude, ere they sank into the deep, waved their fins and their claws, each after his kind, and repeated as with one voice:

"*An ainm an Athar, 's an Mhic, 's an Spioraid Naoimh!*"

And the glory that was upon the Sound of Iona was as though God trailed a starry net upon the waters, with a shining star in every little hollow, and a flowing moon of gold on every wave.

Then Colum the White put out both his arms, and blessed the children of God that are in the deeps of the sea and that are in the deeps of the air.

That is how Sabbath came upon all living things upon Hy that is called Iona, and within the air above Hy, and within the sea that is around Hy.

And the glory is Colum's.

III

THE MOON-CHILD

A YEAR and a day before God bade Colum arise to the Feast of Eternity, Pòl the Freckled, the youngest of the brethren, came to him, on a night of the nights.

"The moon is among the stars, O Colum. By his own will, and yours, old Murtagh that is this day with God, is to be laid in the deep dry sand at the east end of the isle."

So the holy Saint rose from his bed of weariness, and went and blessed the place that Murtagh lay in, and bade neither the creeping worm nor any other creature to touch the sacred dead. "Let God only," he said, "let God alone strip that which he made to grow."

But on his way back sleep passed from him. The sweet salt smell of the sea was in his nostrils; he heard the running of a wave in all his blood.

[171]At the cells he turned, and bade the brethren go in. "Peace be with you," he sighed wearily.

Then he moved downwards to the sea.

A great tenderness, of late, was upon Colum the Bishop. Ever since he had blessed the fishes and the flies, the least of the children of God, his soul had glowed in a whiter flame. There were deep seas of compassion in his gray-blue eyes. One night he had waked, because God was there.

"O Christ," he cried, bowing low his old gray head. "Sure, ah sure, the gladness and the joy, because of the hour of the hours."

But God said: "Not so, Colum, who keepest me upon the Cross. It is Murtagh, Murtagh the druid that was, whose soul I am taking to the glory."

With that Colum rose in awe and great grief. There was no light in his cell. In the deep darkness, his spirit quailed. But lo, the beauty of his heart wrought a soft gleam about him, and in that moonshine of good deeds he rose and made his way to where Murtagh slept.

The old monk slept indeed. It was a [172]sweet breath he drew—he, young and fair now, and laughing with peace under the apples in Paradise.

"O Murtagh," Colum cried, "and thee I thought the least of the brethren, because that thou wast a druid, and loved not to see thy pagan kindred put to the sword if they would not repent. But, true, in my years I am becoming as a boy who learns, knowing nothing. God wash the sin of pride out of my life!"

At that a soft white shining, as of one winged and beautiful, stood beside the dead.

"Art thou Murtagh?" whispered Colum, in deep awe.

"No, I am not Murtagh," came as the breath of vanishing song.

"What art thou?"

"I am Peace," said the glory.

Thereupon Colum sank to his knees, sobbing with joy, for the sorrow that had been and was no more.

"Tell me, O White Peace," he murmured, "can Murtagh hearken there under the apples, where God is?"

"God's love is a wind that blows hitherward [173]and hence. Speak, and thou shalt hear."

Colum spake. "O Murtagh my brother, tell me in what way it is that I still keep God crucified upon the Cross."

There was a sound in the cell as of the morning-laughter of children, of the singing of birds, of the sunlight streaming through the blue fields of Heaven.

Then Murtagh's voice came out of Paradise, sweet with the sweetness: honey-sweet it was, and clothed with deep awe because of the glory.

"Colum, servant of Christ, arise!"

Colum rose, and was as a leaf there, a leaf that is in the wind.

"Colum, thine hour has not yet come. I see it, bathing in the white light which is the Pool of Eternal Life, that is in the abyss where deep-rooted are the Gates of Heaven."

"And my sin, O Murtagh, my sin?"

"God is weary because thou hast not repented."

"O my God and my God! Sure, Murtagh, if that is so, it is so, but it is not for knowledge to me. Sure, O God, it is a [174]blessing I have put on man and woman, on beast and bird and fish, on creeping things and flying things, on the green grass and the brown earth and the flowing wave, on the wind that cometh and goeth, and on the mystery of the flame! Sure, O God, I have sorrowed for all my sins: there is not one I have not fasted and prayed for. Sorrow upon me!—Is it accursed I am, or what is the evil that holdeth me by the hand?"

Then Murtagh, calling through sweet dreams and the rainbow-rain of happy tears that make that place so wondrous and so fair, spake once more:

"O Colum, blind art thou. Hast thou yet repented because that after thou didst capture the great black seal, that is a man under spells, thou, with thy monks, didst crucify him upon the great rock at the place where, long ago, thy coracle came ashore?"

"O Murtagh, favoured of God, will you not be explaining to Him that is King of the Elements, that this was because the seal who was called Black Angus wrought evil upon a mortal woman, and that of the sea-seed was sprung one who had no soul?"

[175]But no answer came to that, and when Colum looked about him, behold there was no soft shining, but only the body of Murtagh the old monk. With a heavy heart, and his soul like a sinking boat in a sea of pain, he turned and went out into the night.

A fine, wonderful night it was. The moon lay low above the sea, and all the flowing gold and flashing silver of the rippling running water seemed to be a flood going that way and falling into the shining hollow splendour.

Through the sea-weed the old Saint moved, weary and sad. When he came to a sandy place he stopped. There, on a rock, he saw a little child. Naked she was, though clad with soft white moonlight. In her hair were brown weeds of the sea, gleaming golden because of the glow. In her hands was a great shell, and at that shell was her mouth. And she was singing this song; passing sweet to hear, it was, with the sea-music that was in it:

> A little lonely child am I
> That have not any soul:
> God made me but a homeless wave,
> Without a goal.
>
> [176] A seal my father was, a seal
> That once was man:
> My mother loved him tho' he was
> 'Neath mortal ban.
>
> He took a wave and drownèd her,
> She took a wave and lifted him:
> And I was born where shadows are
> I' the sea-depths dim.
>
> All through the sunny blue-sweet hours
> I swim and glide in waters green;
> Never by day the mournful shores
> By me are seen.
>
> But when the gloom is on the wave
> A shell unto the shore I bring:
> And then upon the rocks I sit
> And plaintive sing.
>
> O what is this wild song I sing,
> With meanings strange and dim?
> No soul am I, a wave am I,
> And sing the Moon-Child's hymn.

Softly Colum drew nigh.

"Peace," he said. "Peace, little one. Ah, tender little heart, peace!"

The child looked at him with wide sea-dusky eyes.

"Is it Colum the Holy you will be?"

[177] "No, my fawn, my white dear babe: it is not Colum the Holy I am, but Colum the poor fool that knew not God!"

"Is it you, O Colum, that put the sorrow on my mother, who is the Sea-woman that lives in the whirlpool over there?"

"Ay, God forgive me!"

"Is it you, O Colum, that crucified the seal that was my father: him that was a man once, and that was called Black Angus?"

"Ay, God forgive me!"

"Is it you, O Colum, that bade the children of Hy run away from me, because I was a moon-child, and might win them by the sea-spell into the green wave?"

"Ay, God forgive me!"

"Sure, dear Colum, it was to the glory of God, it was?"

"Ay, he knoweth it, and can hear it, too, from Murtagh, who died this night."

"Look!"

And at that Colum looked, and in a moon-gold wave he saw Black Angus, the seal-man, drifting dark, and the eyes in his round head were the eyes of love. And beside the man-seal swam a woman fair to see, and she [178]looked at him with joy, and with joy at the Moon-Child that was her own, and at Colum with joy.

Thereupon Colum fell upon his knees and cried,—

"Give me thy sorrow, wild woman of the sea!"

"Peace to you, Colum," she answered, and sank into the shadow-thridden wave.

"Give me thy death and crucifixion, O Angus-dhu!" cried the Saint, shaking with the sorrow.

"Peace to you, Colum," answered the man-seal, and sank into the dusky quietudes of the deep.

"Ah, bitter heart o' me! Teach me the way to God, O little child," cried Colum the old, turning to where the Moon-Child was!

But lo, the glory and the wonder!

It was a little naked child that looked at him with healing eyes, but there were no seaweeds in her hair, and no shell in the little wee hands of her. For now, it was a male Child that was there, shining with a light from within: and in his fair sunny hair was a [179]shadowy crown of thorns, and in his hand was a pearl of great price.

"O Christ, my God," said Colum, with failing voice.

"It is thine now, O Colum," said the Moon-Child, holding out to him the shining pearl of great price.

"What is it, O Lord my God?" whispered the old servant of God that was now glad with the gladness: "what is this, thy boon?"

"Perfect Peace."

And that is all.
(*To God be the Glory. Amen.*)

THE ANNIR-CHOILLE

WHEN Cathal mac Art, that was called Cathal Gille-Muire, Cathal the Servant of Mary, walked by the sea, one night of the nights in a green May, there was trouble in his heart.

It was not long since he had left Iona. The good St. Colum, in sending the youth to the Isle of Â-rinn, as it was then called, gave him a writing for St. Molios, the holy man who lived in the sea-cave of the small Isle of the Peak, that is in the eastward hollow at the south end of Arran. A sorrow it was to him to leave the fair isle in the west. He had known glad years there—since, in one of the remote isles to the north, he had seen his father slain by a man of Lochlin, and his mother carried away in a galley oared by fierce yellow-haired men. No kith or kin had he but the old priest, that was the brother of his father, Cathal Gille-Chriosd, Cathal the Servant of Christ.

[184]On Iona he had learned the way of Christ. He had a white robe; and could, with a shaven stick and a thin tuft of seal-fur, or with the feather-quill of a wild swan or a solander, write the holy words upon strained lambskin or parchment, and fill the big letters, that were here and there, with earth-brown and sky-blue and shining green, with scarlet of blood and gold of sun-warm sands. He could sing the long holy hymns, too, that Colum loved to hear; and it was his voice that had the sweetest clear-call of any on the island. He was in the nineteenth year of his years when a Frankish prince, who had come to Iona for the blessing of the Saint, wanted him to go back with him to the Southlands. He promised many things because of that voice. Cathal dreamed often, in the hot drowsy afternoons of the month that followed, of the long white sword that would slay so well; and of the white money that might be his to buy fair apparel with, and a great black stallion accoutred with trappings wrought with gold, and a bed of down; and of white hands, and white breasts, and the white song of youth.

[185]He had not gone with the Frankish prince, nor wished to go. But he dreamed often. It was on a day of dream that he lay on his back in the hot grass upon a dune, near where the cells of the monks were. The sun-glow bathed the isle in a golden haze. The strait was a shimmering dazzle, and the blue wavelets that made curves in the soft white sand seem to spill gold flakes and change them straightway into little jets of foam or bubbles of rainbow-spray. Cathal had made a song for his delight. His pain was less when he had made it. Now, lying there, and dreaming at times of the words of the Frankish prince, and remembering at times the stranger words of the old pagan helot, Neis, who had come with him out of the north, he felt fire burn in his veins, and he sang:

> O where in the north, or where in the south, or where in the east or westIs she who hath the flower-white hands and the swandown breast?O, if she be west, or east she be, or in the north or south,A sword will leap, a horse will prance, ere I win to Honey-Mouth.
>> [186]She has great eyes, like the doe on the hill, and warm and sweet she is,O, come to me, Honey-Mouth, bend to me, Honey-Mouth, give me thy kiss!

> *White Hands* her name is, where she reigns amid the princes fair:White hands she moves like swimming swans athrough her dusk-wave hair:White hands she puts about my heart, white hands fan up my breath:White hands take out the heart of me, and grant me life or death!
> White hands make better songs than hymns, white hands are young and sweet:O, a sword for me, O Honey-Mouth, and a war-horse fleet!
> O wild sweet eyes! O glad wild eyes! O mouth, how sweet it is!O, come to me, Honey-Mouth! bend to me, Honey-Mouth! give me thy kiss!

When he had ceased he saw a shadow fall upon the white sand beyond the dune. He looked up, and beheld Colum the Saint.

"Who taught you that song?" said the white holy one, in a voice hard and stern.

"No one, O Colum."

"Then the Evil One is indeed here. Cathal, I promised that you would be having [187]a holy name soon, but that name I will not be giving you now. You must come to me in sackcloth and with dust upon your head, with pain upon you, and with deep grief in your heart. Then only shall I bless you before the brothers and call you Cathal Gille-Mhoire, Cathal the servant of Mary."

A bitter, sad waiting it was for him who had fire in his young blood and was told to weave frost there, and to put silence upon the welling song in his heart. But at the end of the week Cathal was a holy monk again, and sang the hymns that Colum had taught him.

It was on the eve of the day when Colum blessed him before the brethren, and called him Gille-Muire, that he walked alone, brooding upon the evil of women and the curse they brought, and praying to Mary to save him from the sins of which he scarce knew the meaning. On his way back to his cell he passed old Neis, the helot, who said to him mockingly:

"It is a good thing that sorrow, Cathal mac Art,—and yet, sure, it is true that but for the hot love the slain man your father [188]had for Foam that was your mother, you would not be here to praise your God or serve the woman whom the arch-druid yonder says is the Mother of God."

Cathal bade the man eat silence, or it would go ill with him. But the words rankled. That night in his cell he woke, with on his lips his own sinful words:

> White hands make better songs than hymns, white hands are young and sweet;O, a sword for me, O Honey-Mouth, and a war-horse fleet!

On the morrow he went to Colum and told him that the Evil One would not give him peace. That night the Saint bade him make ready to go east to the Isle of Arran—the sole isle, then, where the Pictish folk would let the white robes of the Culdees go scatheless. To the holy Molios he was to go, him that dwelled in the sea-cave of the Isle of the Peak, that men already called the Holy Isle because of the preaching and the miracles of Molios.

"He is a wise man," said Colum to himself, "and he was a pagan Cruithne once, [189]and a prince at that, and he knows the sweetness of sin, and will keep Cathal away from the snares that are set. With fasting, and much peril by day and weariness by night, the blood of the youth will forget the songs the Evil One has put into his mind and it will sing holy hymns. Great will be the glory. Cathal Gille-Muire will be a holy man while he has yet his youth upon him; and he will be a martyr to the flesh by day and by night and by night and by day, till the heathen put him to death because of the faith that is his."

Thus it was that Cathal was blessed by Colum, and sent east among the wild Picts.

It was with joy that he served Molios. For four months he gave him all he had to give. The old saint passed word to Colum that Cathal was a saint and was assured of the crown of martyrdom, and lovingly he urged that the youth should be sent to the Isle of Mist in the north, the great isle that was ruled by Scathach the Queen. There, at the last Summer-sailing, the pagans had flayed a monk alive. A fair happy end: and Cathal was now worthy—and withal [190]might triumph, and might even convert the heathen queen. "She is wondrous fair to see," he added, "and Cathal is a comely youth."

But Colum had answered that the young monk was to bide where he was, and to seek to win souls in the pagan Isle of Arran, where the Cross was still feared.

But with the coming of May and golden weather, the blood of Cathal grew warm. At times, even, he dreamed of the Frankish prince and the evil sweet words he had said.

Then a day of the days came. Molios and Cathal went to a hill-dûn where the Pict chieftain lived, and converted him and all the people in the dûn and all in the rath that was beyond the dûn. That eve the daughter of the warrior came upon Cathal walking in a solitary place, among the green pines beyond the rath. She was most sweet to look upon: tall and fair, with eyes like the sea in a cloudless noon, and hair like westward wheat turned back upon itself.

"What is the name men call you by, young druid?" she said. "I am Ardanna, the daughter of Ecta."

[191]"Your beauty is sweet to look upon, Ardanna. I am Cathal the son of Art the son of Aodh of the race of Alpein, from the isles of the sea. But I am not a druid. I am a priest of Christ, a servant of Mary the Mother of God, and a son of God."

Ardanna looked at him. A flush came into his face. In his eyes the same light flamed that was there when the Frankish prince told him of the delights of the world.

"Is it true, O Cathal, that the druids—that the priests of Christ and the two other gods, the white-robed men whom we call Culdees, and of whom you are one, is it true that they will have nought to do with women?"

Cathal looked upon the woman no more, but on the ground at his feet.

"It is true, Ardanna."

The girl laughed. It was a low, sweet, mocking laugh, but it went along Cathal's blood like cloud-fire along the sky. It was to him as though somewhat he had not seen was revealed.

"And is it a true thing that you holy men [192]look at women askance, and as snares of peril and evil?"

"It is true, Ardanna; but not so upon those who are sisters of Christ, and whose eyes are upon heavenly things."

"But what of those who are not sisters of your god, and are only women, fair to look upon, fair to woo, fair to love?"

Cathal again flushed. His eyes were still upon the ground. He made no answer.

Ardanna laughed low.

"Cathal!"

"Yes, fair daughter of Ecta?"

"Is it never longing for love you are?"

"There is but one love for us who have taken the vows of chastity."

"What is chastity?"

Cathal raised his eyes and glanced at Ardanna. Her dark-blue eyes looked at him pure and sweet, though a smile was upon her mouth. He sighed.

"It is the sanctity of the body, Ardanna."

"I do not understand," she said simply. "But tell me this, poor Cathal—"

"Why do you call me poor Cathal?"

"Because you have put your manhood [193]from you—and you so young, and strong, and comely—and are not a warrior, and care neither for the sword, nor the chase, nor the harp, nor for women."

Cathal was troubled. He looked again and again at Ardanna. The sunset light was in her yellow hair, which was about her as a glory. He had seen the moon as wondrous pale as her beautiful face. Like lilies her white hands were. He had dreamed of that flamelight in the eyes.

"I care," he said.

She drew nearer, and leaned a little forward, and looked at him.

"You are good to look upon, Cathal—the comeliest youth I have ever seen."

The monk flushed. This was the devil-tongue of which Colum had warned him. But how sweet the words were: like a harp that low voice. Sure, sweeter is a waking dream than a dream in sleep.

"I care," he repeated dully.

"Look, Cathal."

Slowly he raised his eyes. As his gaze moved upward it rested on the white breast which was like sea-foam swelling out of [194]brown sea-weed, for she had a tanned fawn-skin belted and gold-claspt over the white robe she wore, and that had disparted for the warm air to play upon her bosom.

It troubled him. He let his eyes fall again. The red was on his face.

"Cathal!"

"Yes, Ardanna."

"And you will never put your kiss upon a woman's lips? Never put your heart upon a woman's heart? Is it of cold sea water you are made—for even the running water in the streams is warmed by the sun? Tell me, Cathal, would you leave Molios the Culdee,—if—"

The monk of Christ suddenly flashed his eyes upon the woman.

"If what, Ardanna?" he asked abruptly: "if what, Ardanna that is so witching fair?"

"If I loved you, Cathal? If I, the daughter of Ecta the chief, loved you, and took you to be my man, and you took me to be your woman, would you be content so?"

He stared at her as one in a dream. Then suddenly all the foolish madness that had been put upon him by Colum fell away. [195]What did these old men, Colum and Molios, know? It is only the young who know what life is. They were old, and their blood was gelid.

He put up his arms, as though in prayer. Then he smiled. Ardanna saw a light in his eyes that sprang into her heart and sang a song there that whirled in her ears and dazzled her eyes and made her feel as though she had fallen over a great height and were still falling.

Cathal was no longer pale. A red flame burned in either cheek. The sunset-light behind him filled his hair with fire. His eyes were beacons.

"Cathal, Cathal!"

"Come, Ardanna!"

That was all. What need to say more. She was in his arms, and her heart throbbing against his that leapt in his body like a wolf fallen in a snare.

He stooped and kissed her. She lifted her eyes, and his brain swung. She kissed him, and he kissed her till she gave a low cry and gently thrust him back. He laughed.

[196]"Why do you laugh, Cathal?"

"I? It is I who laugh now. The old men put a spell upon me. I am no more Cathal Gille-Muire, but Cathal mac Art. Nay, I am Cathal Gille-Ardanna."

With that he plucked the branch of a rowan that grew near. He stripped it of its leaves, and threw them from him north, south, east, and west.

"Why do you do that, Cathal-aluinn?" Ardanna asked, looking at him with eyes of love, and she like a summer morning there, because of the sunshine in her hair, and the wild roses on her face, and the hill-tarn blue of her eyes.

"These are all the hymns that Colum taught me. I give them back. I am knowing them no more. They are idle, foolish songs."

Then the monk took the branch and broke it, and threw the pieces upon the ground and trampled upon them.

"Why do you that, Cathal-aluinn?" asked Ardanna, wondering at him with her home-call eyes.

"That is the branch of all the wisdom [197]Colum taught me. Old Neis, the helot, was wise. It is a madness, all that. See, it is gone: it is beneath my feet: I am a man now."

"But O Cathal, Cathal! this very day of the days, Ecta, my father, has become a man of the Christ-faith, him and his; and he would do what Molios asked, now. And Molios would ask your death."

"Death is a dream."

With that Cathal leaned forward and kissed Ardanna upon the lips twice. "A kiss for life that," he said; "and that a kiss for death."

Ardanna laughed a low laugh. "The monk can kiss," she whispered: "can the monk love?"

He put his arm about her, and they went into the dim dark greenness.

The moon rose slowly, a globe of pale golden fire which spilled unceasingly a yellow flame upon the suspended billows of the forest. Star after star emerged. Deep silence was in the woods, save for the strange, passionate churring of a night-jar, where he leaned low from a pine branch and [198]called to his mate, whose heart throbbed a flight-away amid the dewy shadows.

The wind was still. The white rays of the stars wandered over the moveless, over the shadowless and breathless green lawns of the tree-tops.

"What is that sound?" said Ardanna, a dim shape in the darkness, where she lay in the arms of Cathal.

"I know not," said the youth; for the fevered blood in his veins sang a song against his ears.

"Listen!"

Cathal listened. He heard nothing. His eyes dreamed again into the silence.

"What is that sound?" she whispered against his heart once again. "It is not from the sea, nor is it of the woods."

"It is the moan of Heaven," answered Cathal wearily: "*an acain Pharais*."

II

They found them there in the twilight of the dawn. For long, Ecta looked at them and pondered. Then he glanced at Molios. There were tears in the heart of the holy man, but in his eyes a deep anger.

"Bind him," said Ecta.

Cathal woke with the thongs. His gaze fell upon Molios. He made no sign, and spake never a word: but he smiled.

"What now, O Molios?" asked Ecta.

"Take the woman away. Do with her as you will—spare or slay. It matters not. She is but a woman, and she hath wrought evil upon this man. To slay were well."

"She is my daughter."

"Spare, then, if you will; but take her away. Give her to a man. She shall never see this renegade again."

With that, two men led Ardanna away. She gave a glance at Cathal, who smiled. No tears were in her eyes: but a proud fire was there, and she brooked no man's hand upon her, and walked free.

When she was gone, Molios spake.

"Cathal, that was called Cathal Gille-Muire, why have you done this thing?"

"Because I was weary of vain imaginings, and I am young: and Ardanna is fair, and we loved."

"Such love is death."

"So be it, Molios. Such death is sweet as love."

"No ordinary death shalt thou have, blasphemer. Yet even now I would be merciful if I could. Dost thou call upon God?"

"I call upon the gods of my fathers."

"Fool, they shall not save you."

"Nevertheless, I call. I have nought to do with thy three gods, O Christian."

"Hast thou no fear of hell?"

"I am a warrior, and the son of my father, and of a race of heroes. Why should I fear?"

Molios brooded a while.

"Take him," he said at last, "and bury him alive where his gods perchance will hear his cries and come and save him! Find me a hollow tree."

"There is a great oak near here," said [201]Ecta, wondering, "a great hollow oak whose belly would hold five men, each standing upon the other."

With that he led them to an ancient tree.

"Dost thou repent, Cathal?" Molios asked.

"Ay," the young man answered grimly; "I repent. I repent that I wasted the good days serving you and your three false gods."

"Blaspheme no more. Thou knowest that these three are one God."

Cathal laughed mockingly.

"Hearken to him, Ecta," he cried; "this old druid would have you believe that two men and a woman make one person! Believe that if you will! As for me, I laugh."

But with that, at a sign from Molios, they lifted and slung him amid the branches of the oak, and let him slide feet foremost into the deep hollow heart of the tree.

When the law was done, Molios bade all near kneel in a circle round the oak. Then he prayed for the soul of the doomed man. As he ended this prayer, a laugh flew up among the high wind-swayed leaves. It was [202]as though an invisible bird were there, mocking like a jay.

One by one, with bowed heads, Molios and Ecta and those with him withdrew, all save two young men who were bidden to stay. Upon these was bond laid, that they would not stir from that place for three days. They were to let none draw nigh; and no food was to be given to the victim; and if he cried to them, they were to take no heed,—nay, not though he called upon God or the Mother of God or upon the White Christ.

All that day there was no sound from the hollow tree. At the setting of the sun a blackbird lit upon a small branch that drooped over the aperture, and sang a brave lilt. Then the dark came, and the moon rose, and the stars glimmered through the dew.

At midnight the moon was overhead. A flood of pale gold rays lit up the branches of the oak, and turned the leaves into a lustrous bronze. The watchers heard a voice singing in the silence of the night—a voice muffled and obscure, as from one in a pit, or as that [203]of a shepherd straying in a narrow corrie. Words they caught, though not all; and this was what they heard:[5]

> O yellow lamp of Ioua that is having a cold pale flame there,Put thy honey-sheen upon me who am close-caverned with Death:Sure it is nought I see now who have seen too much and too little:O moon, thy breast is softer and whiter than hers who burneth the day.
>> Put thy white light on the grave where the dead man my father is,And waken him, waken him, wake!And put my soft shining on the breast of the woman my mother,So that she stir in her sleep and say to the Viking beside her,"Take up thy sword, and let it lap blood, for it thirsts with long thirst."

And O Ioua, be as the sea-calm upon the hot heart of Ardanna, the girl:Tell her that Cathal loves her, and that memory is sweeter than life.[204]I list her heart beating here in the dark and the silence,And it is not lonely I am, because of that, and remembrance.

O yellow flame of Ioua, be a spilling of blood out of the heart of Ecta,So that he fall dead, inglorious, slain from within, as a greybeard;And light a fire in the brain of Molios, so that he shall go moonstruck,And men will jeer at him, and he will die at the last, idly laughing.

For lo, I worship thee, Ioua; and if you can give my message to Neis,—Neis the helot out of Aoidû, who is in Iona, bondman to Colum,—Tell him I hail you as Bandia, as god-queen and mighty,And that he had the wisdom and I was a fool with trickling ears of moss.

But grant me this, O goddess, a bitter moon-drinking for Colum! May he have the moonsong in his brain, and in his heart the moonfire:Flame burn him in heart of flame, and may he wane as wax at the furnace,And his soul drown in tears, and his body be a nothingness upon the sands!

> [5] *Ioua* was one of the early Celtic names of the moon. The allusion (in the fourth line) to the sun, in the feminine, is in accordance with ancient usage.

[205]The watchers looked at each other, but said no word. On the pale face of each was fear and awe. What if this new god-teaching were false, and if Cathal was right, and the old gods were the lords of life and death? The moonlight fell upon them, and they saw doubt in the eyes of each other. Neither looked at the white fire. Out of the radiance, cold eyes might stare upon them: and at that, sure they would leap to the woods, laughing wild, and be as the beasts of the forest.

While it was still dark, an hour before the dawn, one of the twain awoke from a brief slumber. His gaze wandered from vague tree to tree. Thrice he thought he saw dim shapes glide from bole to bole or from thicket to thicket. Suddenly he discerned a tall figure, silent as a shadow, standing at the verge of the glade.

His low cry aroused his companion.

"What is it, Mûrta?" the young man asked in a whisper.

"A woman."

When they looked again she was gone.

"It was one of the Hidden People," said [206]Mûrta, with restless eyes roaming from dusk to dusk.

"How are you for knowing that, Mûrta?"

"She was all in green, just like a green shadow she was, and I saw the green fire in her eyes."

"Have you not thought of one that it might be?"

"Who?"

"Ardanna."

With that the young man rose and ran swiftly to the place where he had seen the figure. But he could see no one. Looking at the ground he was troubled: for in the moonshine-dew he descried the imprint of small feet.

Thereafter they saw or heard nought, save the sights and sounds of the woodland.

At sunrise the two youths rose. Mûrta lifted up his arms, then sank upon his knees with bowed head.

"Why do you do that forbidden thing?" said Diarmid, that was his companion. "Have you forgotten Cathal the monk that is up there alone with death? If Molios the holy one saw you worshipping the Light he would do unto you as he has done unto Cathal."

[207]But before Mûrta answered they heard the voice of Cathal once more—hoarse and dry it was, but scarce weaker than when it thrilled them at the rising of the moon.

This was what he chanted in his muffled voice out of his grave there in the hollow oak:

> O hot yellow fire that streams out of the sky, sword-white and golden,Be a flame upon the monks who are praying in their cells in Ioua!Be a fire in the veins of Colum, and the hell that he preacheth be his.And be a torch to the men of Lochlin that they discover the Isle and destroy it!
>
> For I see this thing, that the old gods are the gods that die not:All else is a seeming, a dream, a madness, a tide ever ebbing.Glory to thee, O Grian, lord of life, first of the gods, Allfather.Swords and spears are thy beams, thy breath a fire that consumeth.
>
> And upon this isle of Â-rinn send sorrow and death and disaster,Upon one and all save Ardanna, who gave me her bosom,[208]Upon one and all send death, the curse of a death slow and swordless,From Molios of the Cave to Mûrta and Diarmid my doomsmen!

At that Mûrta moved close to the oak.

"Hail, O Cathal!" he cried. There was silence.

"Art thou a living man still, or is it the death of thee that is singing there in the hollow oak?"

"My limbs perish, but I die not yet," answered the muffled voice that had greeted the sun.

"I am Mûrta mac Mûrta mac Neisa, and my heart is sore for thee, Cathal!"

There was no word to this. A thrush upon a branch overhead lifted its wings, sang a wild sweet note, and swooped arrowly through the green gloom of the leaves.

"Cathal, that wert a monk, which is the true thing? Is it Christ, or the gods of our fathers?"

Silence. Three oaks away a woodpecker thrust its beak into the soft bark, tap-tapping, tap-tapping.

[209]"Cathal, is it death you are having, there in the dark and the silence?"

Mûrta strained his ears, but he could hear no sound. Over the woodlands a voice floated, drowsy-warm and breast-white—the voice of a cuckoo calling a love-note from cool, green shadow to shadow across a league of windless blaze.

Then Mûrta that was a singer, went to where the bulrushes grew by a little tarn that was in the moss an arrow-flight away. He plucked a last-year reed, straight and brown, and with his knife cut seven holes in it. With a thinner reed he scooped the hollow clean.

Thereupon he returned to the oak. Diarmid, who had begun to eat of the food that had been left with them, sat still, with his eyes upon him.

Mûrta put his hollow reed to his lips, and he played. It was a forlorn, sweet air that he had heard from a shepherding woman upon the hills. Then he played a burying-song of the islanders, wherein the wash of the sea and the rippling of the waves upon the shore was heard. Then he played the [210]song of love, and the beating of hearts was heard, and sighs, and a voice like a distant bird-song rose and fell.

When he ceased, a voice came out of the hollow oak—

"Play me a death-song, Mûrta mac Mûrta mac Neisa."

Mûrta smiled, and he played again the song of love.

After that there was silence for a brief while. Then Mûrta played upon his reed for the time it takes a heron to mount her seventh spiral. Then he ceased, and threw away the reed, and stood erect, staring into the greenness. In his eyes was a strange shine. He sang—

> Out of the wild hills I am hearing a voice, O Cathal! And I am thinking it is the voice of a bleeding sword. Whose is that sword? I know it well: it is the sword of the Slayer—Him that is called Death, and the song that it sings I know:—*O where is Cathal mac Art, that is the cup for the thirst of my lips?*

> [211]Out of the cold grayness of the sea I am hearing, O Cathal, I am hearing a wave-muffled voice, as of one who drowns in the depths: Whose is that voice? I know it well: it is the voice of the Shadow—Her that is called the Grave, and the song that she sings I know:—*O where is Cathal mac Art, he has warmth for the chill that I have?*
>
> Out of the hot greenness of the wood I am hearing, O Cathal, I am hearing a rustling step, as of one stumbling blind. Whose is that rustling step? I know it well: the rustling walk of the Blind One—She that is called Silence, and the song that she sings I know:—*O where is Cathal mac Art, that has tears to water my stillness?*

After that there was silence. Mûrta moved away. When he sat by Diarmid and ate, there was no word spoken. Diarmid did not look at him, for he had sung a song of death, and the shadow was upon him. He kept his gaze upon the moss: if he raised his eyes might he not see the Slayer, or the Shadow or the Blind One?

[212]Noon came. None drew nigh: not a face was seen shadowily afar off. Sometimes the hoofs of the deer rustled among the bracken. The snarling of young foxes in an oak-root hollow was like a red pulse in the heat. At times, in the sheer abyss of blue sky to the north, a hawk suspended: in the white-blaze southerly a blotch like swirled foam appeared for a moment at long intervals, as a gannet swung from invisible pinnacles of air to the invisible sea.

The afternoon drowsed through the sunflood. The green leaves grew golden, saturated with light. At sundown a flight of wild doves rose out of the pines, wheeled against the shine of the west and flashed out of sight, flames of purple and rose, of foam-white and pink.

The gloaming came, silverly. The dew glistened on the fronds of the ferns, in the cups of the moss. From glade to glade the cuckoos called. The stars emerged delicately, as the eyes of fawns shining through the greengloom of the forest. Once more the moon snowed the easter frondage of the pines and oaks.

No one came nigh. Not a sound had sighed from the oak since Mûrta had sung at the goldening of the day. At sunset Mûrta had risen, to lean, intent, against the vast bole. His keen ears caught the jar of a beetle burrowing beneath the bark. There was no other sound.

At the fall of dark the watchers heard the confused far noise of a festival. It waned as a lost wind. Dim veils of cloud obscured the moon; a low rainy darkness suspended over the earth.

Thus went the second day and the second night.

When, after the weary vigil of the hours, dawn came at last, Mûrta rose and struck the oak with a stone.

"Cathal!" he cried, "Cathal!"

There was no sound: not a stir, not a sigh.

"Cathal! Cathal!"

Mûrta looked at Diarmid. Then, seeing his own thought in the eyes of his friend he returned to his side.

"The Blind One has been here," said Diarmid in a low voice.

At noon there was thunder, and great heat. The noise of rustling wings filled the underwood.

Diarmid fell into a deep sleep. When the thunder had travelled into the hills, and a soft rain fell, Mûrta climbed into the branches of the oak. He stared down into the hollow, but could see nothing save a green dusk that became brown shadow, and brown shadow that grew into a blackness.

"*Cathal!*" he whispered.

Not a breath of sound ascended like smoke.

"Cathal! Cathal!"

The slow drip of the rain slipped and pattered among the leaves. The cry of a sea-bird flying inland came mournfully across the woods. A distant clang, as of a stricken anvil, iterated from the barren mountain beyond the forest.

"Cathal! Cathal!"

Mûrta broke a straight branch, stripped it of the leaves, and, forcing the thicker end downward, let it fall sheer.

It struck with a dull, soft thud. He listened: there was not a sound.

[215] "A quiet sleep to you, monk," he whispered, and slipped down through the boughs, and was beside Diarmid again.

At dusk the rain ceased. A cool green freshness came into the air. The stars were as wind-whirled fruit blown upward from the tree-tops. The moon, full-orbed and with a pulse of flame, led a tide of soft light across the brown shores of the world.

The vigils of the watchers were over. Mûrta and Diarmid rose. Without a word they moved across the glade: the faint rustle of their feet stirred the bracken: then they left the under-growth and were among the pines. Their shadows lapsed into the obscure wilderness. A doe, heavy with fawn, lay down among the dewy fern, and was at peace there.

[216]

III

At midnight, when the whole isle lay in the full flood of the moon, Cathal stirred.

For three days and three nights he had been in that dark hollow, erect, wedged as a spear imbedded in the jaws of a dead beast. He had died thrice: with hunger, with thirst, with weariness. Then when hunger was slain in its own pain, and thirst perished of its own agony, and weariness could no more endure, he stirred with the death-throe.

"I die," he moaned.

"Die not, O white one," came a floating whisper, he knew not whence, though it was to him as though the crushing walls of oak breathed the sound.

"I die," he gasped, and the froth bubbled upon his nether lip. With that his last strength went. No more could he hold his head above his shoulder, nor would his feet sustain him. Like a stricken deer he sank. So thin was he, so worn, that he slipt into a narrow crevice where dead leaves had been, and lay there, drowning in the dark.

Was that death, or a cold air about his feet, he wondered? With a dull pain he moved them: they came against no tree-wood—the coolness about them was of dewy moss. A wild hope flashed into his mind. With feeble hands he strove to sink farther into the crevice.

"I die," he gasped, "I die now, at the last."

"Die not, O white one," breathed the same low sweet whisper, like leaves stirred by a nesting bird.

"Save, O save," muttered the monk, hoarse with the death-dew.

Then a blackness came down upon him from a great height, and he swung in that blank gulf as a feather swirled this way and that in the void of an abyss.

When the darkness lifted again, Cathal was on his back, and breathing slow, but without pain. A sweet wonderful coolness and ease, that he knew now! Where was he? he wondered. Was he in that Pàras that Colum and Molios had spoken of? Was he in Hy Bràsil, of which he had heard Aodh the Harper sing? Was he in Tir-na'n-Òg, where all men and women are young for evermore, and there is joy in the heart and peace in the mind and delight by day and by night?

Why was his mouth so cool, that had burned dry as ash? Why were his lips moist, with a bitter-sweet flavour, as though the juice of fruit was there still?

He pondered, with closed eyes. At last he opened them, and stared upward. The profound black-blue dome of the sky held group after group of stars that he knew: was not that sword and belt yonder the sword-gear of Fionn? Yon shimmering cluster, were they not the dust of the feet of Alldai? That leaping green and blue planet, what could it be but the harp of Brigidh, where she sang to the gods?

A shadow crossed his vision. The next moment a cool hand was upon his eyes. It brought rest, and healing. He felt the blood move in his veins: his heart beat: a throbbing was in his throat.

Then he knew that he had strength to rise. With a great effort he put his weariness from off him, and staggered to his feet.

Cathal gave a low sob. A fair beautiful woman stood by him.

"Ardanna!" he cried, though even as the word leaped from his lips he knew that he looked upon no Pictish woman.

She smiled. All his heart was glad because of that. The light in her eyes was like the fire of the moon, bright and wonderful. The delicate body of her was pale green, and luminous as a leaf, with soft earth-brown hair falling down her shoulders and over the swelling breast; even as the small green mounds over the dead the two breasts were. She was clad only in her own loveliness, though the moonshine was about her as a garment.

"Like a green leaf, like a green leaf," Cathal muttered over and over below his breath.

"Are you a dream?" he asked simply, having no words for his wonder.

"No, Cathal, I am no dream. I am a woman."

"A woman? But ... but ... you have no body as other women have: and I see the moonbeam that is on your breast shining upon the moss behind you!"

"Is it thinking you are, poor Cathal, that there are no women and no men in the world except those who are in thick flesh, and move about in the suntide."

Cathal stared wonderingly.

"I am of the green people, Cathal. We are of the woods. I am a woman of the woods."

"Hast thou a name, fair woman?"

"I am called Deòin."[6]

> [6] *Deo-uaine.*

"That is well. Truly 'Green Life' is a good name for thee. Are there others of thy kin in this place?"

"Look!" and at that she stooped, lifted the dew of a white flower in the moonshine, and put it upon his eyes.

Cathal looked about him. Everywhere he saw tall fair pale-green lives moving to and fro: some passing out of trees, swift and silent as rain out of a cloud; some passing into trees, silent and swift as shadows. All were fair to look upon: tall, lithe, graceful, moving this way and that in the moonshine, pale green as the leaves of the lime, soft [221]shining, with radiant eyes, and delicate earth-brown hair.

"Who are these, Deòin?" Cathal asked in a low whisper of awe.

"They are my people: the folk of the woods: the green people."

"But they come out of trees: they come and they go like bees in and out of a hive."

"Trees? That is your name for us of the woods. *We* are the trees."

"*You* the trees, Deòin! How can that be?"

"There is life in your body. Where does it go when the body sleeps, or when the sap rises no more to heart or brain, and there is chill in the blood, and it is like frozen water? Is there a life in your body?"

"Ay, so. I know it."

"The flesh is *your* body: the tree is *my* body."

"Then you are the green life of a tree?"

"I am the green life of a tree."

"And these?"

"They are as I am."

"I see those that are men and those that are women, and their offspring too I see."

[222]"They are as I am."

"And some are crowned with pale flowers."

"They love."

"And hast thou no crown, Deòin, who art so fair?"

"Neither hast thou, Cathal, though thy face is fair. Thy body I cannot see, because thou hast a husk about thee."

With a low laugh Cathal removed his raiment from him. The whiteness of his body was like a flower there in the moonshine.

"That shall not be against me," he said. "Truly I am a man no longer, if thee and thine will have me as one of the wood-folk."

At that Deòin called. Many green phantoms glided out of the trees, and others, hand-in-hand, flower-crowned, crossed the glade.

"Look, green lives," Deòin cried in her sweet leaf-whisper, rising now like a wind-song among birchen boughs: "Look, here is a human. His life is mine, for I saved him. I have put the moonshine dew upon his eyes. He sees as we see. He would be one of us, for all that he has no tree for his body, but flesh, white over red."

[223]One who had moved thitherward out of an ancient oak looked at Cathal.

"Wouldst thou be of the wood-folk, man?"

"Ay, fain am I; for sure, for sure, O druid of the trees."

"Wilt thou learn and abide by our laws, the first of which is that none may stir from his tree until the dusk has come, nor linger away from it when the dawn opens gray lips and drinks up the shadows?"

"I have no law now but the law of green life."

"Good. Thou shalt live with us. Thy home shall be the hollow oak where thy kin left thee to die. Why did they do that evil deed?"

"Because I did not believe in the new gods."

"Who are thy gods, man whom this green one here calls Cathal?"

"They are the Sun, and the Moon, and the Wind, and others that I will tell you of."

"Hast thou heard of Keithoir?"

"No."

"He is the god of the green world. He dreams, and his dreams are Springtide and Summertide and Appletide. When he sleeps without dream there is winter."

"Have you no other god but this earth-god?"

"Keithoir is our god. We know no other."

"If he is thy god, he is my god."

"I see in the eyes of Deòin that she loves thee, Cathal the human. Wilt thou have her love?"

Cathal looked at the girl. His heart swam in light.

"Ay, if Deòin will give me her love, my love shall be hers."

The Annir-Choille moved forward, and brushed softly against him as a green branch.

He put his arms around her. She had a cool, sweet body to feel. He was glad she was no moonshine phantom. The beating of her heart against his made a music that filled his ears.

Deòin stooped and plucked white, dewy flowers. Of these she wove a wreath for Cathal. He, likewise, plucked the white blooms, and made a coronal of foam for the brown wave of her hair.

Then, hand in hand, they fared slowly forth across the moonlit glade. None crossed their path, though everywhere delicate green lives flitted from tree to tree. They heard a wonderful sweet singing, aerial, with a ripple as of leaves lipping a windy shore of light. A green glamour was in the eyes of Cathal. The green fire of life flamed in his veins.

IV

Molios, the saint of Christ, that lived in the sea-cave of the Isle of the Peak, so that even in his own day it was called the Holy Isle, endured to a great age.

Some say of him that before his hair was bleached white as the bog-cotton, he was slain by the heathen Picts, or by the fierce summer-sailors out of Lochlin. But that is an idle tale. His end was not thus. A Culdee, who had the soul of a bat, feared the truth, though that gave glory to God, and wrote both in ogham and lambskin the truthless tale that Molios went forth with the cross and was slain in a north isle.

On a day of the days every year, Molios fared to the Hollow Oak that was in the hill-forest beyond the rath of Ecta mac Ecta. There he spake long upon the youth that had been his friend, and upon how the Evil One had prevailed with Cathal, and how the islander had been done to death there in the oak. Then he and all his company sang the hymns of peace, and great joy there was [227]over the doom of Cathal the monk, and many would have cleft the great tree or burned it, so that the dust of the sinner might be scattered to the four winds: only this was banned by Molios.

It was well for Cathal, who slept there through the hours of light! Deep slumber was his, for never once did he hear the noontide voices, nor ever in his ears was the long rise and fall of the holy hymns.

But when, in the twentieth year after Cathal had been thrust into the hollow oak, Molios came at sundown, being weary with the heat, the saint heard a low, faint laughter issuing from the tree, like fragrance from a flower.

None other heard it. He saw that with gladness. Quietly he went with the islanders.

When the moon was over the pines, and all in the rath slept, Molios arose and went silently back into the forest.

When he came to the Doom-Tree he listened long, with his ear against the bark. There was no sound.

His voice was old and quavering, but fresh and young in the courts of heaven, when it [228]reached there like a fluttering bird tired from long flight. He sang a holy hymn.

He listened. There was no laughter. He was glad at that. All had been a dream, for sure.

Then it was that he heard once again the low, mocking laughter. He started back, trembling.

"Cathal!" he cried, with his voice like a wuthering wind.

"I am here, O Molios," said a voice behind him.

The old Culdee turned, as though arrow-nipped. Before him, white in the moonshine, stood a man, naked.

At first Molios knew him not. He was so tall and strong, so fair and wonderful. Long locks of ruddy hair hung upon his white shoulders: his eyes were lustrous, and had the lovely, soft light of the deer. When he moved, it was swiftly and silently. No stag upon the hills was more fair to see.

Then, slowly, Cathal the monk swam into Cathal of the Woods. Molios saw him whom he knew of old, as a blue flame is visible within the flame of yellow.

[229]"I am here, O Molios."

Strange was the voice: faint and far the tone of it: yet it was that of a living man.

"Is it a spirit you are, Cathal?"

"I am no spirit. I am Cathal the monk that was, Cathal the man now."

"How came you out of hell, you that are dead, and the dust of whose crumbling bones is in the hollow of this oak?"

"There is no hell, Culdee."

"No hell!" Molios the Saint stared at the wood-man in blank amaze.

"No hell!" he said again; "and is there no heaven?"

"A hell there is, and a heaven there is: but not what Colum taught, and you taught."

"Doth Christ live?"

"I know not."

"And Mary?"

"I know not."

"And God the Father?"

"I know not."

"It is a lie that you have upon your lips. Sure, Cathal, you shall be dead indeed soon, to the glory of God. For I shall have thy dust scattered to the four winds, and thy [230]bones consumed in flame, and a stake be driven through the place where thou wast."

Once more Cathal laughed.

"Go back to the sea-cave, Molios. Thou hast much to learn. Brood there upon the ways of thy God before thou judgest if He knoweth no more than thou dost. And see, I will show you a wonder. Only, first, tell me this one thing. What of Ardanna whom I loved?"

"She was accursed. She would not believe. When Ecta took the child from her, that was born in sin, to have the water put upon it with the sign of the Cross, she went north beyond the Hill of the Pinnacles. There she saw the young king of the Picts of Argyll, and he loved her, and she went to his dûn. He took her to his rath in the north, and she was his queen. He, and she, and the two sons she bore to him are all under the hill-moss now: and their souls are in hell."

Cathal laughed, low and mocking.

"It is a good hell that, I am thinking, Molios. But come ... I will show you a wonder."

With that he stooped, and took the [231]moonshine dew out of a white flower, and put it upon the eyes of the old man.

Then Molios saw.

And what he saw was a strangeness and a terror to him. For everywhere were green lives, fair and comely, gentle-eyed, lovely, of a soft shining. From tree to tree they flitted, or passed to and fro from the tree-boles, as wild bees from their hives.

Beside Cathal stood a woman. Beautiful she was, with eyes like stars in the gloaming. All of green flame she seemed, though the old monk saw her breast rise and fall, and the light lift of her earth-brown hair by a wind-breath eddying there, and the hand of her clasped in that of Cathal. Beyond her were fair and beautiful beings, lovely shapes like unto men and women, but soulless, though loving life and hating death, which, of a truth, is all that the vain human clan does.

"Who is this woman, Cathal?" asked the saint, trembling.

"It is Deòin, whom I love, and who has given me life."

"And these ... that are neither green [232]phantoms out of trees, nor yet men as we are?"

"These are the offspring of our love."

Molios drew back in horror.

But Cathal threw up his arms, and with glad eyes cried:

> "O green flame of life, pulse of the world.O Love! O Youth! O Dream of Dreams."

"O bitter grief," Molios cried, "O bitter grief, that I did not slay thee utterly on that day of the days! Flame to thy flesh, and a stake through thy belly—that is the doom thou shouldst have had! My ban upon thee, Cathal, that was a monk, and now art a wild man of the woods: upon thee, and thy Annir-Coille, and all thy brood, I put the ban of fear and dread and sorrow, a curse by day and a curse by night!"

But with that a great dizziness swam into the brain of the saint, and he fell forward, and lay his length upon the moss, and there was no sight to his eyes, or hearing to his ears, or knowledge upon him at all until the rising of the sun.

When the yellow light was upon his face [233]he rose. There was no face to see anywhere. Looking in the dew for the myriad feet that had been there, he saw none.

The old man knelt and prayed.

At the first praying God filled his heart with peace. At the second praying God filled his heart with wonder. At the third praying God whispered mysteriously, and he knew. Humble in his new knowledge, he rose. The tears were in his old eyes. He went up to the Hollow Oak, and blessed it, and the wild man that slept within it, and the Annir-Coille that Cathal loved, and the offspring of their love. He took the curse away, and he blessed all that God had made.

All the long weary way to the shore he went as one in a dream. Wonder and mystery were in his eyes.

At the shore he entered the little coracle that brought him daily from the Holy Isle, a triple arrow-flight seaward.

A child sat in it, playing with pebbles. It was Ardan, the son of Ardanna.

"Ardan mac Cathal," began the saint, weary now, but glad with a strange new gladness.

[234]"Who is Cathal?" said the boy.

"He that was thy father. Tell me, Ardan, hast thou ever seen aught moving in the woods—green lives out of the trees?"

"I have seen a green shine come out of the trees."

Molios bowed his head.

"Thou shalt be as my son, Ardan; and when thou art a man thou shalt choose thy own way, and let no man hinder thee."

That night Molios could not sleep. Hearing the loud wash of the sea, he went to the mouth of the cave. For a long while he watched the seals splashing in the silver radiance of the moonshine. Then he called them.

"O seals of the sea, come hither!"

At that all the furred swimmers drew near.

"Is it for the curse you give us every year of the years, O holy Molios?" moaned a great black seal.

"O Ròn dubh, it is no curse I have for thee or thine, but a blessing, and peace. I have learned a wonder of God, because of an Annir-Coille in the forest that is upon the [235]hill. But now I will be telling you the white story of Christ."

So there, in the moonshine, with the flowing tide stealing from his feet to his knees, the old saint preached the gospel of love. The seals crouched upon the rocks, with their great brown eyes filled with glad tears.

When Molios ceased, each slipped again into the shadowy sea. All that night, while he brooded upon the mystery of Cathal and the Annir-Coille, with deep knowledge of hidden things, and a heart filled with the wonder and mystery of the world, he heard them splashing to and fro in the moon-dazzle, and calling, one to the other, "We, too, are the sons of God."

At dawn a shadow came into the cave. A white frost grew upon the face of Molios. Still was he, and cold, when Ardan, the child, awoke. Only the white lips moved. A ray of the sun slanted across the sea, from the great disc of whirling golden flame new risen. It fell softly upon the moving lips. They were still then, and Ardan kissed them because of the smile that was there.

[237]

THE SHADOW-SEERS

[239]

I

THE SIGHT[7]

[7] These four short episodes are reprinted, by courteous consent of the Editor of *Harper's Magazine*, where they appeared, interpolated in "From the Hebrid Isles."

THE "vision," or second-sight, is more common in the Western Isles than in the Highlands; now at least, when all things sacred to the Celtic race, from the ancient language to the degenerate and indeed all but vanished Beltane and Samh'in rites, are smiled at by the gentle and mocked by the vulgar. A day will come when men will lament more what is irrecoverable than ever a nation mourned for lapsed dominion. It is a bitter cruel thing that strangers must rule the hearts and brains, as well as the poor fortunes, of the mountaineers and islanders. Yet in doing their best to thrust Celtic life and speech and thought into the sea, they are working a sore hurt for themselves that they shall discern in the day of adversity. We of the passing race know this thing: that in a day to come the sheep-runs shall not be in the Isles and the Highlands only—for we see the forests moving south, and there will be lack, then, not of deer and of sheep, but of hunters and shepherds.

That which follows is only a memento of what was told me last summer by a fisherman of Iona. If I were to write all I have heard about what is called second-sight, it would be a volume and not a few pages I should want. The "sight" has been a reality to me almost from the cradle, for my Highland nurse had the faculty, and I have the memory of more than one of her trances.

There is an old man on the island named Daibhidh (David) Macarthur.[8] It was Ivor McLean, my boatman friend, who took me [241]to him. He is a fine old man, though "heavy" a little; with years, perhaps, for his head is white as the crest of a wave. He is one of the very few of Iona, perhaps of the two or three at most, who do not speak any English.

> [8] As there are several Macarthurs on Iona, I may say that the old man I allude to was not so named. Out of courtesy I disguise his name: though, since the above was written, he is no more.

"No," he told me, "he had never had the sight himself. Ivor was wrong in saying that he had."

This, I imagine, was shyness, or, rather, that innate reticence of the Celt in all profoundly intimate and spiritual matters; for, from what Ivor told me, I am convinced that old Macarthur had more than once proved himself a seer.

But he admitted that his wife had "it."

We were seated on an old upturned boat on the rocky little promontory, where once were first laid the innumerable dead, brought for burial to the sacred soil of Iona. For a time Macarthur spoke slowly about this and that; then, abruptly and without preamble, he told me this:

The Christmas before last, Mary, his wife, had seen a man who was not on the island. [242]"And that is true, by St. Martin's Cross," he added.

They were, he said, sitting before the fire, when, after a long silence, he looked up to see his wife staring into the shadow in the ingle. He thought she was brooding over the barren womb that had been her life-long sorrow, and now in her old age had become a strange and gnawing grief, and so he turned his gaze upon the red coals again.

But suddenly she exclaimed, *"C'ait am bheil thu dol?"* (Where are you going?)

He looked up, but saw no one in the room beside themselves.

"What has come to you?" he asked. "What do you see?"

But she took no notice.

"C'uine tha thu falbh?" (When are you going?) she muttered, with the same strained voice and frozen eyes. And then, once again, *"C'uine thig thu rithisd?"* (When will you come again?) And with that she bowed her head, and the thin backs of the hands upon her knees were wet with falling tears.

For the fourth of an hour thereafter she would say nothing except moan, *"Tha an amhuinn domhain; tha an amhuinn domhain; fuar, fuar; domhain, domhain!"*[9] (Deep, deep is the river; cold and deep; cold and deep!)

[9] Pronounce Ha aun ah-ween do'-inn; fēw-ar, fēw-ar; do'-inn, do'-inn.

And the man she saw, added Macarthur, was her nephew, Luthais, in Cape Breton, of Nova Scotia, who, as they learned before Easter, was drowned that Christmas-tide. He was the last of his mother's race, and had been the foster-child of Mary.

II

THE DARK HOUR OF FERGUS

IN September of last year I was ferried across the Sound of Kerrera by an old boatman.

That afternoon I went with my friend, a peasant farmer near the south end of Kerrera, and lay down in the grassy, bouldered wilderness beneath the cliff on which stands the ruin of Gylen Castle. The tide called in a loud insistent whisper, rising to a hoarse gurgle, from the Sound. The breeze that came from the mountains of Mull was honey-sweet with heather smell. The bleating of the ewes and lambs, the screaming of a few gulls,—nothing else was audible. At times, it is true, like a deep sigh, the suspiration of the open sea rose and fell among the islands. Faint echoes of that sigh came round Gylen headland and up the Kyle. It was an hour wherein to dream of the sons of Morven, who had landed here often, long before the ancient [245]stronghold was built; of Fionn and the Féinn of the coming and going of Ossian in his blind old age; of beautiful Malvina; of the galleys of the Fomorians; of the songs and the singers and all the beautiful things of "the old ancient long ago."

But the tale that I heard from my friend was this:

You know that my mother's people are Skye folk. It was from the mother of my mother that I heard what you call the Incantation of the Spirit, though I never heard it called anything but old Elsie's *Sian*. She lived near the Hart o' Corry. You know the part? Ay, true, it is wild land—wild even for the wilderness o' Skye. Old mother Elsie had "the sight" at times, and whenever she wished she could find out the lines o' life. It was magic, they say. Who am I to know? This is true, she knew much that no one else knew. When my mother's cousin, Fergus MacEwan, who was mate of a sloop that sailed between Stornoway and Ardrossan, came to see her—and that was in the year before my mother was married, and when she [246]was courted by Fergus, though she was never for giving her life to him, for even then she loved my father, poor fisherman of Ulva though he was (though heir, through his father's brother, to his crofter-farm on Kerrera here)—when Fergus came to see her, because of the gloom that was upon his spirit, she foretold all. At first she could "see" poorly. But one wild afternoon, when the Cuchullins were black with cloud-smoke, she bade him meet her in that lonely savage glen they call the Loat o' Corry. He was loath to go, for he feared the place. But he went. He told all to my mother before he went away next dawn, with the heart in him broken, and his hope as dead as a herring in a net.

Mother Elsie came to him out of the dusk in that wuthering place just like a drifting mist, as he said. She gave him no greeting, but was by his side in silence. Before he knew what she was doing she had the soles of her feet upon his, and her hands folding his, and her eyes burning against his like hot coals against ash. He felt shudders come over him, and a wind blew up and down his back; [247]and he grew giddy, and heard the roaring of the tides in his ears. Then he was quiet. Her voice was very far away when she said this thing, but he remembered every word of it:

> By that which dwells within thee,By the lamps that shine upon me,By the white light I see littenFrom the brain now sleeping stilly,By the silence in the hollows,By the wind that slow subsideth,By the life-tide slowly ebbing,By the deith-tide slowly rising,By the slowly waning warmth,By the chill that slowly groweth,By the dusk that slowly creepeth,By the darkness near thee,By the darkness round thee,By the darkness o'er thee—O'er thee, round thee, on thee—By the one that standethAt thy side and waitethDumb and deaf and blindly,By the one that moveth,Bendeth, raiseth, watcheth,By the dim Grave-Spell upon thee,By the Silence thou hast wedded....May the way thy feet are treading,May the tangled lines now crookèd,Clear as moonlight lie before me!
>
> [248]*Oh! oh! ohrone, ochrone! green the branches bonnie:Oh! oh! ohrone! ochrone! red the blood-drop berries:Achrone, arone, arone, arone, I see the green-clad Lady.She walks the road that's wet with tears, with rustling sorrows shady....Oh! oh! mo ghraidh.*

Then it was that a great calm came upon Fergus, though he felt like a drowned man, or as one who stood by his own body, but speechless, and feeling no blowing of wind through his shadow-frame.

For, indeed, though the body lived, he was already of the company of the silent. What was that *caiodh*, that wailing lamentation, sad as the *Cumha fir Arais*, which followed Elsie's incantation, her spell upon "the way" before him, that it and all the trailed lines of this life should be clear as moonlight before her? *Oh! oh! ohrone, ochrone! red the blood-drop berries*; did not these mean no fruit of the quicken-tree, but the falling drops from the maimed tree that was himself? And was not the green-clad lady, she who comes singing low, the sprouting of the green grass that is the hair of the earth? And was not the road, gleaming wet with ruts and pools all of tears, and overhung by dark rustling plumes of sorrow, the road that the soul traverses in the dark hour? And did not all this mean that the Grave Spell was already upon him, and that the Silence was to be his?[10]

> [10] (1) *Caiodh* (a wailing lament) is a difficult word to pronounce. The Irish *keen* will help the foreigner with *Kúë-yh* or *Kúë-yhn*. (2) The *Cumha fir Arais* (pronounce *Kŭv'ah feer Arooss*) means the lament of the man of Aros—*i. e.*, the chieftain. Aros Castle, on the great island of Mull, overlooking the Sound, was one of the strongholds of Macdonald, Lord of the Isles. (3) The quicken (rowan, mountain-ash, and other names) is a sacred tree with the Celtic peoples, and its branches can either avert or compel supernatural influences. (4) The green-clad Lady is the Cailleach, the Siren of the Hill-Sides, to see whom portends death or disaster. When she is heard singing, that portends death soon for the hearer. The grass is that which grows quick and green above the dead. The dark hour is the hour of death—*i. e.*, the first hour after death.

But what thing it was she saw, Elsie would not say. Darkly she dreamed awhile, then leaned forward and kissed his breast. He felt the sob in her heart throb into his.

Dazed, and knowing that she had seen more than she had dreamed of seeing, and that his hour was striding over the rocky wilderness of that wild Isle of Skye, he did not know she was gone, till a shuddering fear of the silence and the gloom told him he was alone.

Coll MacColl (he that was my Kerrera friend) stopped here, just as a breeze will suddenly stop in a corrie so that the rowan berries on the side of a quicken will sway this way and that, while the long thin leaves on the other will be as still as the stones underneath, where their shadows sleep.

I asked him at last if Elsie's second-sight had proved true. He looked at me for a moment, as though vaguely surprised I should ask so foolish a thing.

No sleep came to Fergus that night, he resumed, quietly, as though no other words were needed, and at daybreak he rose and left the cot of his kinsman, Andrew MacEwan. In the gray dawn he saw my mother, and told her all. Then she [251]wished him farewell, and bade him come again when next the *Sunbeam* should be sailing to Portree, or other port in Skye; for she did not believe that her mother had seen speedy death, or death at all, but perhaps only a time of sorrow, and even that she had done this thing to send Fergus away, for she too had her eyes on Robert MacColl, that was my father.

"And so you will come again, Fergus my friend," she said; and added, "and perhaps then you will be telling me of a Sunbeam ashore, as well as that you sail from Ardrossan to the far away islands!"

He stared at her as one who hears ill. Then he took her hand in his, and let it go suddenly again. With one arm he rubbed the rough Uist cap he held in his left hand; then he brushed off the wet mist that was gray on his thick black beard.

"You are not well, Fearghas-mo-charaid," my mother said, and gently. When she saw the staring pain in his eyes, she added, with a low sob, "My heart is sore for you!"

With that he turned away, and she saw [252]him no more, that day or any day of all the days to come.

"And what thing happened, Coll?"

"They kept it from her, and she did not know it for long. It was this: Fergus McEwan did not sail far that morning. He was ill, he said, and was put ashore. That night Aulay Macaulay saw him moving about in that frightful place of the Storr Rock, moaning and muttering. He would have spoken to him, but he saw him begin to leap about the pinnacled rocks like a goat, and at last run up to The Old Man of Storr and beat it with his clinched fists, blaspheming with wild words; and he feared Fergus was mad, and he slipped from shadow to shadow, till he fled openly. But in the morning Aulay and his brother Finlay went back to look for Fergus. At first they thought he had been drowned, or had fallen into one of the fissures. But from a *balachan*, a 'bit laddie,' as they would call him in the town over the way [Oban], they heard that a man had pushed off that morning in John Macpherson's boat, that lay about a mile and a half from the Storr, and had sailed north along the coast.

[253]"Well, it was three days before he was found—stone-dead. If you know the Quiraing you will know the great Needle Rock. Only a bird can climb it, as the saying goes. Half-way up, Finlay Macaulay and a man of the neighbourhood saw the body o' Fergus as though it were glued to the rock. It was windless weather, for he would have blown away like a drifted leaf. They had to jerk the body down with net-poles. God save us the dark hour of Fergus, that died like a wild beast!"

[254]

III

THE WHITE FEVER

ONE night, before the peats, I was told this thing by old Cairstine Macdonald, in the isle of Benbecula. It is in her words that I give it:

In the spring of the year that my boy Tormaid died, the moon-daisies were as thick as a woven shroud over the place where Giorsal, the daughter of Ian, the son of Ian MacLeod of Baille 'n Bad-a-sgailich, slept night and day.[11]

> [11] *Baille 'n Bad-a-sgailich*: the Farm of the Shadowy Clump of Trees. *Cairstine*, or *Cairistine*, is the Gaelic for *Christian*, as *Tormaid* is for Norman, and *Giorsal* for Grace. "The quiet havens" is the beautiful island phrase for graves. Here, also, a swift and fatal consumption that falls upon the doomed is called "The White Fever." By "the mainland," Harris and Lewis are meant.

All that March the cormorants screamed, famished. There were few fish in the sea, [255]and no kelp-weed was washed up by the high tides. In the island and in the near isles, ay, and far north through the mainland, the blight lay. Many sickened. I knew young mothers who had no milk. There are green mounds in Carnan kirk-yard that will be telling you of what this meant. Here and there are little green mounds, each so small that you might cuddle it in your arm under your plaid.

Tormaid sickened. A bad day was that for him when he came home, weary with the sea, and drenched to the skin, because of a gale that caught him and his mates off Barra Head. When the March winds tore down the Minch, and leaped out from over the Cuchullins, and came west, and lay against our homes, where the peats were sodden and there was little food, the minister told me that my lad would be in the quiet havens before long. This was because of the white fever. It was of that same that Giorsal waned, and went out like a thin flame in sunlight.

The son of my man (years ago weary no more) said little ever. He ate nothing [256]almost, even of the next to nothing we had. At nights he couldna sleep because of the cough. The coming of May lifted him awhile. I hoped he would see the autumn; and that if he did, and the herring came, and the harvest was had, and what wi' this and what wi' that, he would forget his Giorsal that lay i' the mools in the quiet place yonder. Maybe then, I thought, the sorrow would go, and take its shadow with it.

One gloaming he came in with all the whiteness of his wasted body in his face. His heart was out of its shell; and mine, too, at the sight of him.[12]

> [12] *A cochall a' chridhe*: his heart out of its shell—a phrase often used to express sudden derangement from any shock. The ensuing phrase means the month from the 15th of July to the 15th of August, *Mios crochaidh nan con*, so called as it is supposed to be the hottest if not the most waterless month in the isles. The word *claar* used below, is the name given a small wooden tub, into which the potatoes are turned when boiled.

This was in the season of the hanging of the dog's mouth.

"What is it, Tormaid-a-ghaolach?" I asked, with the sob that was in my throat.

"*Thraisg mo chridhe*," he muttered (my [257]heart is parched). Then, feeling the asking in my eyes, he said, "I have seen her."

I knew he meant Giorsal. My heart sank. But I wore my nails into the palms of my hands. Then I said this thing, that is an old saying in the isles: "Those who are in the quiet havens hear neither the wind nor the sea." He was so weak he could not lie down in the bed. He was in the big chair before the peats, with his feet on a *claar*.

When the wind was still I read him the Word. A little warm milk was all he would take. I could hear the blood in his lungs sobbing like the ebb-tide in the sea-weed. This was the thing that he said to me:

"She came to me, like a gray mist, beyond the dyke of the green place, near the road. The face of her was gray as a gray dawn, but the voice was hers, though I heard it under a wave, so dull and far was it. And these are her words to me, and mine to her—and the first speaking was mine, for the silence wore me:

> Am bheil thu' falbh,O mo ghraidh?B'idh mi falbh,Mùirnean!
> [258]C'uin a thilleas tu,O mo ghraidh?Cha till mi an rathad so;Tha an't ait e cumhann—O mùirnean, mùirnean!B'idh mi falbh an drùghAm tigh Pharais,Mùirnean!
> Sèol dhomh an rathad,Mo ghraidh!Thig an so Mùirnean-mo,Thig an so!

> Are you going, My dear one? *Yea, now I am going, Dearest.*
> When will you come again, My dear one? *I will not return this way; The place is narrow—O my darling! I will be going to Paradise, Dear, my dear one!*
> Show me the way, Heart of my heart! *Come hither, dearest, come hither, Come with me!*

"And then I saw that it was a mist, and that I was alone. But now this night it is that I feel the breath on the soles of my feet."

And with that I knew there was no hope. "*Ma tha sin an dàn!* ... if that be ordained," was all that rose to my lips. It was that night he died. I fell asleep in the second hour. When I woke in the gray dawn, his face was grayer than that and more cold.

IV

THE SMOOTHING OF THE HAND

GLAD am I that wherever and whenever I listen intently I can hear the looms of Nature weaving Beauty and Music. But some of the most beautiful things are learned otherwise—by hazard, in the Way of Pain, or at the Gate of Sorrow.

I learned two things on the day when I saw Sheumas McIan dead upon the heather. He of whom I speak was the son of Ian McIan Alltnalee, but was known throughout the home straths and the countries beyond as Sheumas Dhu, Black James, or, to render the subtler meaning implied in this instance, James the Dark One. I had wondered occasionally at the designation, because Sheumas, if not exactly fair, was not dark. But the name was given to him, as I learned later, because, as commonly rumoured, he knew that which he should not have known.

[261]I had been spending some weeks with Alasdair McIan and his wife Silis (who was my foster-sister), at their farm of Ardoch, high in a remote hill country. One night we were sitting before the peats, listening to the wind crying amid the corries, though, ominously as it seemed to us, there was not a breath in the rowan-tree that grew in the sun's-way by the house. Silis had been singing, but silence had come upon us. In the warm glow from the fire we saw each others' faces. There the silence lay, strangely still and beautiful, as snow in moonlight. Silis's song was one of the *Dana Spioradail*, known in Gaelic as the Hymn of the Looms. I cannot recall it, nor have I ever heard or in any way encountered it again.

It had a lovely refrain, I know not whether its own or added by Silis. I have heard her chant it to other runes and songs. Now, when too late, my regret is deep that I did not take from her lips more of those sorrowful strange songs or chants, with their ancient Celtic melodies, so full of haunting sweet melancholy, which she loved so well. It was with this refrain that, after a long stillness, [262]she startled us that October night. I remember the sudden light in the eyes of Alasdair McIan, and the beat at my heart, when, like rain in a wood, her voice fell unawares upon us out of the silence:

> *Oh! oh! ohrone, arone! Oh! Oh! mo ghraidh, mo chridhe! Oh! oh! mo ghraidh, mo chridhe!*[13]
>
> > [13] Pronounce mogh-rāy, mogh-rēe (my heart's delight
> > —*lit.*, my dear one, my heart).

The wail, and the sudden break in the second line, had always upon me an effect of inexpressible pathos. Often that sad wind-song has been in my ears, when I have been thinking of many things that are passed and are passing.

I know not what made Silis so abruptly begin to sing, and with that wailing couplet only, or why she lapsed at once into silence again. Indeed, my remembrance of the incident at all is due to the circumstance that shortly after Silis had turned her face to the peats again, a knock came to the door, and then Sheumas Dhu entered.

"Why do you sing that lament, Silis, sister [263]of my father?" he asked, after he had seated himself beside me, and spread his thin hands against the peat glow, so that the flame seemed to enter within the flesh.

Silis turned to her nephew, and looked at him, as I thought, questioningly. But she did not speak. He, too, said nothing more, either forgetful of his question, or content with what he had learned or failed to learn through her silence.

The wind had come down from the corries before Sheumas rose to go. He said he was not returning to Alltnalee, but was going upon the hill, for a big herd of deer had come over the ridge of Mel-Mòr. Sheumas, though skilled in all hill and forest craft, was not a sure shot, as was his kinsman and my host, Alasdair McIan.

"You will need help," I remember Alasdair Ardoch saying, mockingly, adding, "*Co dhiubh is fhearr let mise thoir sealladh na fàileadh dhiubh?*"— that is to say, Whether would you rather me to deprive them of sight or smell?

This is a familiar saying among the old sportsmen in my country, where it is [264]believed that a few favoured individuals have the power to deprive deer of either sight or smell, as the occasion suggests.

"*Dhuit ciàr nan carn!*—The gloom of the rocks be upon you!" replied Sheumas, sullenly; "mayhap the hour is come when the red stag will sniff at my nostrils."

With that dark saying he went. None of us saw him again alive.

Was it a forewarning? I have often wondered. Or had he sight of the shadow?

It was three days after this, and shortly after sunrise, that, on crossing the south slope of Mel Mòr with Alasdair Ardoch, we came suddenly upon the body of Sheumas, half submerged in a purple billow of heather. It did not, at the moment, occur to me that he was dead. I had not known that his prolonged absence had been noted, or that he had been searched for. As a matter of fact, he must have died immediately before our approach, for his limbs were still loose, and he lay as a sleeper lies.

Alasdair kneeled and raised his kinsman's head. When it lay upon the purple tussock, the warmth and glow from the sunlit ling gave a fugitive deceptive light to the pale face. I know not whether the sun can have any chemic action upon the dead. But it seemed to me that a dream rose to the face of Sheumas, like one of those submarine flowers that are said to rise at times and be visible for a moment in the hollow of a wave. The dream, the light, waned; and there was a great stillness and white peace where the trouble had been. "It is the Smoothing of the Hand," said Alasdair McIan, in a hushed voice.

Often I had heard this lovely phrase in the Western Isles, but always as applied to sleep. When a fretful child suddenly falls into quietude and deep slumber, an isles-woman will say that it is because of the Smoothing of the Hand. It is always a profound sleep, and there are some who hold it almost as a sacred thing, and never to be disturbed.

So, thinking only of this, I whispered to my friend to come away; that Sheumas was dead weary with hunting upon the hills; that he would awake in due time.

McIan looked at me, hesitated, and said nothing. I saw him glance around. A few yards away, beside a great boulder in the heather, a small rowan stood, flickering its featherlike shadows across the white wool of a ewe resting underneath. He moved thitherward slowly, plucked a branch heavy with scarlet berries, and then, having returned, laid it across the breast of his kinsman.

I knew now what was that passing of the trouble in the face of Sheumas Dhu, what that sudden light was, that calming of the sea, that ineffable quietude. It was the Smoothing of the Hand.

SEANACHAS[14]

THE SONG OF THE SWORD.

THE FLIGHT OF THE CULDEES.

MIRCATH.

THE LAUGHTER OF SCATHACH THE QUEEN.

> [14] The word "Seanachas" means either traditionary lore, or "telling of tales of the olden time"—and it is in this sense that it is used here.

THE SONG OF THE SWORD

THESE are of the Seanachas told me by Ian Cameron ("Ian Mòr"), before the flaming peats, at a hill-shealing, in a season when the premature snows found the bracken still golden and the ptarmigan with their autumn browns no more than flecked and mottled with gray.

He has himself now a quieter sleep than the sound of that falling snow, and it is three years since his face became as white and as cold.

He had pleasure in telling *sgeul* after *sgeul* of the ancient days. Far more readily at all times would he repeat stories of this dim past he loved so well than the more intimate tales which had his own pulse beating in them, as "The Daughter of the Sun" and others that I have given elsewhere. Often he would look up from where he held his face in his hands as he brooded into the [272]dull steadfast flame that consumed the core of the peats; and without preamble, and with words in no apparent way linked to those last spoken, would narrate some brief episode, and always as one who had witnessed the event. Sometimes, indeed, these brief tales were like waves: one saw them rise, congregate, and expand in a dark billow—and the next moment there was a vanishing puff of spray and the billow had lapsed.

I cannot recall many of these fugitive tales—seanachas, as he spoke of them collectively, for each *sgeul* was of the past, and had its roots in legendary lore—but of those that remained with me, here are four. All came upon me as birds flying in the dark: I knew not whence they came or upon what wind they had steered their mysterious course. They were there, that was all. Ancient things come again in Ian's brain: or recovered out of the dim days, and seen anew through the wonder-lens of his imagination.

[273]It was in a white June, as they call it, in the third year after the pirates of Lochlin had fed the corbies of the Hebrid Isles, that the summer-sailors once more came down the Minch of Skye.

An east wind blew fresh from the mountains, though between dawn and sunrise it veered till it chilled itself upon the granite peaks of the Cuchullins, and then leaped north-westward with the white foam of its feet caught from behind by the sun-glint.

The vikings on board the *Svart-Alf* laughed at that. The spray flew from the curved black prow of the great galley, and the wake danced in the dazzle—the sea-cream that they loved to see.

Tall men they were, and comely. Their locks of yellow or golden or ruddy hair, sometimes braided, sometimes all acurl like a chestnut-tree bud-breaking in April, sometimes tangled like sea-wrack caught in a whirl of wind and tide, streamed upon their shoulders. In their blue eyes was a shining as though there were torches of white flame behind them: and that shining was mild or fierce as home or blood filled their brain.

The *Svart-Alf* was the storm-bird of a fleet of thirty galleys which had set forth from Lochlin under the raven-banner of Olaus the White. The vikings had joyed in a good faring. Singing south winds had blown them to the Faroe Isles, where from Magnus Cleft-Hand they had good cheer, and the hire of three men who knew the Western Isles and had been with the sea-kings who had harried them here and there again and again.

From Magnus-stead they went forth swelled with mead and ale and cow-beef: and they laughed because of what they would give in payment on their way back with golden torques and bracelets and other treasure, young slaves, women dark and fair, and the jewel-hilted weapons of the island-lords.

Cold black winds out of the north-east drove them straight upon the Ord of Sutherland. They sang with joy the noon when they rounded Cape Wrath and came under the shadow of the hills. The dawn that followed was red not only in the sky but on the sheen of the sword-blades. It was the Song of the Sword that day, and there is no song like that for the flaming of the blood. The dark men of Torridon were caught unawares. For seven days thereafter the corbies and ravens glutted themselves drinking at red pools beside the stripped bodies which lay stark and stiff upon the heather. The firing of a score of homesteads smouldered till the rains came, a day and two nights after the old women who had been driven to the moors stole back wailing. The maids and wives were carried off in the galleys: and for nine days, at a haven in the lone coast opposite the Summer Isles, their tears, their laughter, their sullen anger, their wild gaiety, their passionate despair gave joy to the yellow-haired men. On the ninth day they were carried southward on the summer-sailing. At a place called Craig-Feeach, Raven's Crag, in the north of Skye, where a Norse Erl had a great Dûn that he had taken from the son of a king from Eirèann whose sea-nest it had been, Olaus the White rested awhile. The women were left there as a free spoil: save three who were so fair that Olaus kept one, and Haco and Sweno his chief captains took the others.

Then, on an evening when the wind was from the north, Olaus and ten galleys went down the sound. Sweno the Hammerer was to strike across the west for the great island that is called Lewis: Haco the Laugher was to steer for the island that is called Harris: and Olaus himself was to reach the haven called Ljotr-wick in the Isle of the Thousand Waters that is Benbecula.

On the eve of the day following that sailing a wild wind sprang up, blowing straight against the north. All of the south-faring galleys save one made for haven, though it was a savage coast which lay along the south of Skye. In the darkness of the storm Olaus thought that the other nine wave-steeds were following him, and he drove before the gale, with his men crouching under the lee of the bulwarks, and with Finnleikr the Harper singing a wild song of sea-foam and flowing blood and the whirling of swords.

The gale was nigh spent three hours after dawn: but the green seas were like snow-crowned hillocks that roll in earth-drunkenness when the flames surge from blazing mountains. Olaus knew that no boat could [277]live in that sea, except it went before the wind. So, though not a galley was in sight, he fared steadily westward.

By sundown the wind had swung out of the south into the east: and by midnight the stars were shining clear. In the blue-dark could be seen the white wings of the fulmars, seaward-drifting once again from the rocks whither they had fled.

Then came the dawn when the sun-rain streamed gladly, and a fresh east wind blew across the Minch, and the *Svart-Alf*, that had been driven far northward, came leaping south-westwardly, with laughter and fierce shining of sky-blue eyes, where the vikings toiled at the oars, or burnished their brine-stained swords and javelins.

All day they fared joyously thus. Behind them they could see the blue line of the mainland and the dark-blue mountain-crests of Skye: southward was a long green film, where Coll caught the waves ere they drove upon Tiree; south-eastward, the gray-blue peaks of Halival and Haskival rose out of the Isle of Terror, as Rùm was then called. Before them, as far as they could see to [278]north or south, the purple-gray lines that rose out of the west were the contours of the Hebrides.

"Dost thou see yonder blue splatch, Morna?" cried Olaus the White to the woman who lay indolently by his side, and watched the sun-gold redden the mass of ruddy hair which she had sprayed upon the boards, a net wherein to mesh the eyes of the vikings, "do you see that blue splatch? I know what it is. It is the headland that Olaf the Furious called Skipness. Behind it is a long fjord in two forks. At the end of the south fork is a place of the white-robes whom the islanders call Culdees. Midway on the eastern bend of the north fork is a town of a hundred families. Over both rules Maoliosa, a warrior-priest, and under him, at the town, is a graybeard called Rumun mac Coag. All this I have learned from Anlaf the Swarthy, who came with us out of Faroe."

Morna glanced at him under her drooped eyelids. Sure, he was fair to see, for all that his long hair was white. White it had gone with the terror of a night on an ice-floe, [279]whereon a man who hated the young erl had set him adrift with seven wolves. He had slain three, and drowned three, and one had leaped into the sea: and then he had lain on the ice, with snow for a pillow, and in the dawn his hair was the same as the snow. This was but ten years ago, when he was a youth.

She looked at him, and when she spoke it was in the slow lazy speech that in his ears was drowsy-sweet as the hum of the hives in the steading where his home was.

"It will be a red sleep the men of that town will be having soon, I am thinking, Olaus. And the women will not be carding wool when the moon rises to-morrow night. And ..."

The fair woman stopped suddenly. Olaus saw her eyes darken.

"Olaus!"

"I listen."

"If there is a woman there that you desire more than me I will give her a gift."

Olaus laughed.

"Keep your knife in your girdle Morna. Who knows but you may need it soon to save yourself from a Culdee!"

[280]"Bah. These white-robed men-women have nought to do with us. I fear no man, Olaus: but I have a blade for the woman who will dazzle your eyes."

"Have no fear, white wolf. The sea-wolf knows his mate when he has found her!"

An hour after sun-setting a mist came up. The wind freshened. Olaus made silence throughout the war-galley. The vikings had muffled their oars, for the noise of the waves on the shore could now be heard. Hour after hour went by. When, at last, the moonlight tore a rift in the häar, and suddenly the vapour was licked up by a wind moving out of the north, they saw that they were close upon the land, and right eastward of the headland of Skipness.

Anlaf the Swarthy went to the prow. Blackly he loomed in the moonlight as he stood there, poising his long spear, and sounding the depths while the vessel slowly forged shoreward. By the time a haven was found, and the vikings stood silent upon the rocks, the night was yellow with moonshine, and the brown earth overlaid with a soft [281]white sheen wherein the long shadows lay palely blue.

There was deep peace in the island-town. The kye were in the sea-pastures near, and even the dogs slept. There had been no ill for long, and Rumun mac Coag was an old man, and dreamed overmuch about his soul. This was because of the teaching of the Culdees. Before he had known he had a soul he was a man, and would not have been taken unawares—and he over-lord of a sea-town like Bail'-tiorail.

Olaus the White made a wide circuit with his men. Then, slowly, the circle narrowed.

A bull lowed, where it stood among the sea-grass, stamping uneasily, and ever and again sniffing the air. Suddenly one heifer, then another, then all the kye, began a strange lowing. The dogs rose, with bristling felts, and crawled sidelong, snarling, with red eyes gleaming savagely.

Bethoc, the young third wife of Rumun, was awake, dreaming of a man out of Eirèann who had that day given her a strange pleasure with his harp and his dusky eyes. She knew that lowing. It was the *langanaich an* [282]*aghaidh am allamharach*, the continued lowing against the stranger. She rose lightly, and unfastened the leather flap, and looked down from the grianan where she was. A man stood there in the shadow. She thought it was the harper. With a low sigh she leaned downward to kiss him, and to whisper a word in his ear.

Her long hair fell over her eyes and face and blinded her. She felt it grasped, and put out her hand. It was seized, and before she knew what was come upon her she was dragged prone upon the man.

Then, in a flash, she saw he had yellow hair, and was clad as a Norseman. She gasped. If the sea-rovers were come, it was death for all there. The man whispered something in a tongue that was strange to her. She understood better when he put his arm about her, and placed a hand upon her mouth.

Bethoc stood silent. Why did no one hear that lowing of the kine, that snarling of the dogs which had now grown into a loud continuous baying? The man by her side thought she was cowed, or had accepted the change of fate. He left her, and put his foot in a cleft. Then, sword under his chin, he began to climb stealthily.

He had thrown his spear upon the ground. Soundlessly Bethoc stepped forward, lifted it, and moved forward like a shadow.

A wild cry rang through the night. There was a gurgling and spurting sound as of dammed water adrip. Rumun sprang from his couch, and stared out of the aperture. Beneath he saw a man, speared through the back, and pinned to the soft wood. His hands claspt the frayed deer-skins, and his head lay upon his shoulder. He was laughing horribly. A bubbling of foam frothed continuously out of his mouth.

The next moment Rumun saw Bethoc. He had not time to call to her before a man slipped out of the shadow, and plunged a sword through her till the point dripped red drops upon the grass beyond where she stood. She gave no cry, but fell as a gannet falls. A black shadow darted across the gloom. A crash, a scream, and Rumun sank inert, with an arrow fixed midway in his head through the brows.

Then there was a fierce tumult everywhere. From the pastures the kye ran lowing and bellowing, in a wild stampede. The neighing of horses broke into screams. Here and there red flames burst forth, and leapt from hut to hut. Soon the whole rath was aflame. Round the dûn of Rumun a wall of swords flashed.

All had taken refuge in the dûn, all who had escaped the first slaying. If any leaped forth, it was upon a viking spear, or if the face of any was seen it was the targe for a swift-sure arrow.

A long penetrating wail went up. The Culdees, on the further loch, heard it, and ran from their cells. The loud laughter of the sea-rovers was more dreadful to them than the whirling flames and the wild screaming lament of the dying and the doomed.

None came forth alive out of that dûn, save three men, and seven women that were young. Two of the men were made to tell all that Olaus the White wanted to know. Then they were blinded, and put in a boat, and set in the tide-eddy that would take them to where the Culdees were. And, for the Culdees, they had a message from Olaus.

[285]Of the seven women none was so fair that Morna had any heed. But seven men had them as spoil. Their wild keening had died away into a silence of blank despair long before the dawn. When the light came, they were huddled in a white group near the ashes of their homes. Everywhere the dead sprawled.

At sunrise the vikings held an ale-feast. When Olaus the White had drunken and eaten, he left his men and went down to the shore to look upon the fortified place where Maoliosa the Culdee and his white-robes lived. As he fared thither through what had been Bail'-tiorail there was not a male left alive save the one prisoner who had been kept, Aongas the Bow-maker as he was called: none save Aongas, and a strayed child among the salt grasses near the shore, a little boy, naked and with blue eyes and laughing sunny smile.

[289]

THE FLIGHT OF THE CULDEES

ON the wane of noon, on the day following the ruin of Bail'-tiorail, sails

were descried far east of Skipness.

Olaus called his men together. The boats coming before the wind were doubtless his own galleys which he had lost sight of when the south-gale had blown them against Skye: but no man can know when and how the gods may smile grimly, and let the swords that whirl be broken or the spears that are flat become a hedge of death.

An hour later, a startled word went from viking to viking. The galleys in the offing were the fleet of Sweno the Hammerer. Why had he come so far southward, and why were oars so swift and with the stained sails distended before the wind?

They were soon to know.

Sweno himself was the first to land. A man he was, broad and burly, with a sword-slash across his face that brought his brows together in a frown which made a perpetual dusk above his savage blood-shot eyes.

In a few words he told how he had met a galley, with only half its crew, and of these many who were wounded. It was the last of the fleet of Haco the Laugher. A fleet of fifteen war-birlinns had set out from the Long Island, and had given battle. Haco had gone into the strife laughing loud as was his wont, and he and all his men had the berserk rage, and fought with joy and foam at the mouth. Never had the Sword sang a sweeter song.

"Well," said Olaus the White, grimly, "well: how did the Raven fly?"

"When Haco laughed for the last time, with waving sword out of the death wherein he sank, there was only one galley left. Of all that company of vikings there were no more than nine to tell the tale. These nine we took out of their boat, which was below waves soon. Haco and his men are all fighting the sea-shadows by now."

A loud snarling went from man to man. This became a wild cry of rage. Then savage shouts filled the air. Swords were lifted up against the sky, and the fierce glitter of the blue eyes and the bristling of the tawny beards were fair to see, thought the captive women, though their hearts beat against their ribs like eaglets against the bars of a cage.

Sweno the Hammerer frowned a deep frown when he heard that Olaus was there with only the *Svart-Alf* out of the galleys which had gone the southward way.

"If the islanders come upon us now with their birlinns we shall have to make a running fight," he said.

Olaus laughed.

"Aye, but the running shall be after the birlinns, Sweno."

"I hear that there are fifty and nine men, of these Culdees yonder, under the sword-priest Maoliosa?"

"It is a true word. But to-night, after the moon is up, there shall be none."

At that, all who heard laughed, and were less heavy in their hearts because of the slaying and drowning of Haco the Laugher and all his crew.

"Where is the woman Brenda that you took?" Olaus asked, as he stared at Sweno's boat and saw no woman there.

"She is in the sea."

Olaus the White looked. It was his eyes that asked.

"I flung her into the sea because she laughed when she heard of how the birlinns that were under Somhairle the Renegade drave in upon our ships and how Haco laughed no more, and the sea was red with Lochlin blood."

"She was a woman, Sweno—and none more fair in the isles, after Morna that is mine."

"Woman or no woman I flung her into the sea. The Gael call us *Gall*: then I will let no Gael laugh at the Gall. It is enough. She is drowned. There are always women: one here, one there—it is but a wave blown this way or that."

At this moment a viking came running across the ruined town with tidings. Maoliosa and his Culdees were crowding into a great birlinn. Perhaps they were coming to give battle: mayhap they were for sailing away from that place.

Olaus and Sweno stared across the fjord. At first they knew not what to think. If Maoliosa thought of battle he would scarce choose that hour and place. Or was it that he knew the Gael were coming in force, and that the vikings were caught in a trap?

At last it was clear. Sweno gave a great laugh.

"By the blood of Odin," he cried, "they come to sue for peace!"

Slowly across the loch the birlinn, filled with white-robed Culdees, drew near. At the prow stood a tall old man, with streaming hair and beard, white as sea-foam. In his right hand he grasped a great Cross, whereon was Christ crucified.

The vikings drew close one to the other.

"Hail them in their own tongue, Sweno," said Olaus.

The Hammerer moved to the water-edge, as the birlinn stopped, a short arrow-flight away.

"Ho, there, priests of the Christ-faith!"

"What would you, viking?" It was Maoliosa himself that spoke.

"Why do you come here among us, you that are Maoliosa?"

"To win you and yours to God, pagan."

"Is it madness that is upon you, old man? We have swords and spears here, if we lack hymns and prayers."

All this time Olaus kept a wary watch inland and seaward, for he feared that Maoliosa came because of an ambush.

Truly the old monk was mad. He had told his Culdees that God would prevail, and that the pagans would melt away before the Cross.

The ebb-tide was running swift. Even while Sweno spoke, the birlinn touched a low sea-hidden ledge of rock.

A cry of consternation went up from the white-robes. Loud laughter came from the vikings.

"Arrows!" cried Olaus.

With that three score men took their bows. There was a hail of death-shafts. Many fell into the water, but some were in the brains and hearts of the Culdees.

Maoliosa himself stood in death, transfixed to the mast.

With a wild cry the monks swept their oars backward. Then they leaped to their feet and changed their place, and rowed for life or death.

The summer-sailors sprang into their galley. Sweno the Hammerer was at the bow. The foam curled and hissed.

The birlinn grided upon the opposite shore at the selfsame moment when Sweno brought down his battle-axe upon the monk who steered. The man was cleft to the shoulder. Sweno swayed with the blow, stumbled, and fell headlong into the sea. A Culdee thrust at him with an oar, and pinned him among the sea-tangle. Thus died Sweno the Hammerer.

Then all the white-robes leaped upon the shore. Yet Olaus was quicker than they. With a score of vikings he raced to the Church of the Cells, and gained the sanctuary. The monks uttered a cry of despair, and, turning, fled across the moor. Olaus counted them. There were now forty in all.

"Let forty men follow," he cried.

Like white birds, the monks fled this way and that. Olaus and those who watched laughed at them as they stumbled because of their robes. One by one fell, sword-cleft or spear-thrust. The moorland was red.

At the last there were less than a score—twelve only—ten!

"Bring them back!" Olaus shouted.

When the ten fugitives were captured and brought back, Olaus took the crucifix that Maoliosa had raised, and held it before each in turn. "Smite," he said to the first monk. But the man would not. "Smite!" he said to the second: but he would not. And so it was to the tenth.

"Good," said Olaus the White: "they shall witness to their god." With that he bade his vikings break up the birlinn, and drive the planks into the ground, and shore them up with logs.

When this was done he crucified each Culdee. With nails and with ropes he did unto each what their god had suffered. Then all were left there, by the water-side.

That night, when Olaus the White and the laughing Morna left the great bonfire where the vikings sang and drank horn after horn of strong ale, they stood and looked across the loch. In the moonlight, upon the dim verge of the further shore, they could discern ten crosses. On each was a motionless white splatch.

MIRCATH

The *Mire Chath* was the name given to the war-frenzy that often preceded and accompanied battle.

WHEN Haco the Laugher saw the islanders coming out of the west in their birlinns, he called to his vikings: "Now of a truth we shall hear the Song of the Sword!"

The ten galleys of the Summer-Sailors spread out into two lines of five boats, each boat an arrow-flight from those on either side.

The birlinns came on against the noon. In the sun-dazzle they loomed black as a shoal of pollack. There were fifteen in all, and from the largest, midway among them, flew a banner. On this banner was a disc of gold.

"It is the Banner of the Sunbeam," shouted Olaf the Red, who with Torquil the One-Armed was hero-man to Haco. "I know it well. The Gael who fight under that are warriors indeed."

"Is there a saga-man here?" cried Haco. At that a great shout went up from the vikings: "Harald the Smith!"

A man rose among the bow-men in Olaf's boat. It was Harald. He took a small square harp, and he struck the strings. This was the song he sang:

> Let loose the hounds of war,The whirling swords!Send them leaping afar,Red in their thirst for war;Odin laughs in his carAt the screaming of the swords!
>
> Far let the white-ones fly,The whirling swords!Afar off the ravens spyDeath-shadows cloud the sky.Let the wolves of the Gael die'Neath the screaming swords!
>
> The Shining Ones yonderHigh in ValhallaShout now, with thunder.*Drive the Gaels under,Cleave them asunder—Swords of Valhalla!*

A shiver passed over every viking. Strong men shook as a child when lightning plays. [303]Then the trembling passed. The mircath, the war-frenzy, came on them. Loud laughter, went from boat to boat. Many tossed the great oars, and swung them down upon the sea, splashing the sun-dazzle into a yeast of foam. Others sprang up and whirled their javelins on high, catching them with bloody mouths: others made sword-play, and stammered thick words through a surf of froth upon their lips. Olaf the Red towered high on the steering-plank of the *Calling Raven*, swirling round and round a mighty battle-axe: on the *Sea-Wolf*, Torquil One-Arm shaded his eyes, and screamed hoarsely wild words that no one knew the meaning of. Only Haco was still for a time. Then he, too, knew the mircath: and he stood up in the *Red-Dragon* and laughed loud and long. And when Haco the Laugher laughed, there was ever blood and to spare.

The birlinns of the islanders drave on apace. They swayed out into a curve, a black crescent there in the gold-sprent blue meads of the sea. From the great birlinn that carried the Sunbeam came a chanting voice:

> [304]O 'tis a good song the sea makes when blood is on the wave,And a good song the wave makes when its crest o' foam is red!For the rovers out of Lochlin the sea is a good grave,And the bards will sing to-night to the sea-moan of the dead!Yo-ho-a-h'eily-a-yo, eily, ayah, a yo!Sword and Spear and Battle-axe sing the Song of Woe.Ayah, eily, a yo!Eily, ayah, a yo!

Then there was a swirling and dashing of foam. Clouds of spray filled the air from the thresh of the oars.

No man knew aught of the last moments ere the birlinns bore down upon the viking-galleys. Crash and roar and scream: and a wild surging: the slashing of swords, the whistle of arrows, the fierce hiss of whirled spears, the rending crash of battle-axe and splintering of the javelins, wild cries, oaths, screams, shouts of victors and yells of the dying, shrill taunts from the spillers of life and savage choking cries from those drowning in the bloody yeast, that bubbled and [305]foamed in the maelstrom where the war-boats swung and reeled this way and that—and over all the loud death-music of Haco the Laugher.

Olaf the Red went into the sea, red indeed, for the blood streamed from head and shoulders and fell about him as a scarlet robe. Torquil One-Arm fought, blind and arrow-sprent, till a spear went through his neck, and he sank among the dead. Louder and louder grew the fierce shouts of the Gael: fewer the savage screaming cries of the vikings. Thus it was till two galleys only held living men. The *Calling Raven* turned and fled, with the nine men who were not wounded to the death. But on the *Red Dragon* Haco the Laugher still laughed. Seven men were about him. These fought in silence.

Then Toscar mac Aonghas that was leader of the Gael took his bow. None was arrow-better than Toscar of the Nine Battles. He laid down his sword and took his bow, and an arrow went through the right eye of Haco the Laugher. He laughed no more. The seven died in silence. Swaran Swift-foot [306]was the last. When he fell he wiped away the blood that streamed over his face.

"*Skoal!*" he cried to the hero of the Gael, and with that he whirled his battle-axe at Toscar mac Aonghas: and the soul of Toscar met his, in the dark mist, and upon the ears of both fell at one and the same time the glad laughter of the gods in Valhalla.

[309]

THE LAUGHTER OF SCATHACH THE QUEEN

Scathach (pronounced Scá-ya or Ský-ya) was an Amazonian queen of the Isle of Skye, and is supposed to have given her name to that island.

IN the year when Cuchullin left the Isle of Skye, where Scathach the warrior-Queen ruled with the shadow of death in the palm of her sword-hand, there was sorrow because of his beauty. He had fared back to Eiré, at the summons of Concobar mac Nessa, Ard-Righ of Ulster. For the Clan of the Red Branch was wading in blood, and there were seers who beheld that bitter tide rising and spreading.

Cuchullin was only a youth in years: but he had come to Skye a boy, and he had left it a man. None fairer had ever been seen of Scathach or of any woman. He was tall and lithe as a young pine: his skin was as white as a woman's breast: his eyes were of a fierce bright blue, with a white light in them as of the sun. When bent, and with arrow half-way drawn, he stood on the heather, listening against the belling of the [310]deer; or when he leaned against a tree, dreaming not of eagle-chase or wolf-hunt, but of the woman whom he had never met; or when, by the dûn, he played at sword-whirl or spear-thrust, or raced the war-chariot across the machar—then, and ever, there were eyes upon his beauty and there were some who held him to be Angus Ogue himself. For there was a light about him, such as the hills have in the sun-glow an hour before set. His hair was the hair of Angus and of the fair gods: earth-brown shot with gold next his head, ruddy as flame midway, and, where it sprayed into a golden mist of fire, yellow as windy sunshine.

But Cuchullin loved no woman upon Skye, and none dared openly to love Cuchullin, for Scathach's heart yearned for him, and to cross the Queen was to put the shroud upon oneself. Scathach kept an open face for the son of Lerg. There was no dark frown above the storm in her eyes when she looked at his sunbright face. Gladly she slew a woman because Cuchullin had lightly reproved the maid for some idle thing: and once, when the youth had looked in grave [311]silence at three viking-captives whom she had spared because of their comely manhood, she put her sword through the heart of each, and sent him the blade, dripping red, as the flower of love.

But Cuchullin was a dreamer, and he loved what he dreamed of, and that woman was not Scathach, nor any of her warrior-women who made the Isle of Mist a place of terror for those cast upon the wild shores, or stranded there in the ebb of inglorious battle.

Scathach brooded deep upon her vain desire. Once, in a windless shadowy gloaming, she asked him if he loved any woman.

"Yes," he said, "Etáin."

Her breath came quick and hard. It was for pleasure to her then to think of Cuchullin lying white at her feet, with the red blood spilling from the whiteness of his breast. But she bit her underlip, and said quietly:

"Who is Etáin?"

"She is the wife of Mídir."

And with that the youth turned and moved haughtily away. She did not know that the Etáin of whom Cuchullin dreamed was no woman that he had seen in Eiré, but the [312]wife of Mídir the King of Faerie, who was so passing fair that Mac Greine, the beautiful god, had made for her a grianan all of shining glass, where still she lives in a dream, and in that sun-bower still is fed at dawn upon the bloom of flowers and at dusk upon their fragrance. *O ogham mhic Gréine, tha e boidheach*,[15] she sighs for ever in her sleep: and that sigh is in all sighs of love for ever and ever.

> [15] "O beauty of my love the Sun-lord" (*lit.* "O Youth, son of the Sun, how fair he is!")

Scathach watched him till he was lost behind the flare of the camp-fires of the rath. For long she stood there, brooding deep; till the sickle of the new moon, which had been like a blown feather over the sun as it sank, stood out in silvershine against the blue-black sky, now like a wake in the sea because of the star-dazzle that was there. And what the queen brooded upon was this: whether to send emissaries to Eirèann, under bond to seek in that land till they found Mídir and Etáin, and to slay Mídir and bring to her the corpse, for a gift from her to lay before Cuchullin: or to bring Etáin [313]to Skye, where the Queen might see her lose her beauty and wane into death. Neither way might win the heart of Cuchullin. The dark tarn of the woman's mind grew blacker with the shadow of that thought.

Slowly she moved dûn-ward through the night. "As the moon sometimes is seen rising out of the east," she muttered, "and sometimes, as now, is first seen in the west, so is the heart of love. And if I go west, lo the moon may rise along the sunway: and if I go east, lo the moon may be a white light over the setting sun. And who that knoweth the heart of man or woman can tell when the moon of love is to appear full-orbed in the east or sickle-wise in the west?"

It was on the day following that tidings came out of Eirèann. An Ultonian brought a sword to Cuchullin from Concobar the Ard-righ.

"The sword has ill upon it, and will die, unless you save it, Cuculain son of Lerg," said the man.

"And what is that ill, Ultonian?" asked the youth.

"It is thirst."

[314]Then Cuchullin understood.

On the night of his going none looked at Scathach. She had a flame in her eyes.

At moonrise, she came back into the rath. No one, meeting her, looked in her face. Death lay there, like the levin behind a cloud. But Maev her chief captain sought her, for she had glad news.

"I would slay you for that glad news, Maev," said the Dark Queen to the warrior-woman, "for there is no glad news unless it be that Cuchullin is come again: only, I spare, for you saved my life that day the summer-sailors burned my rath in the south."

Nevertheless, Scathach had gladness because of the tidings. Three viking-galleys had been driven into Loch Scavaig, and been dashed to death there by the whirling wind and the narrow furious seas. Of the ninety men who had sailed in them, only a score had reached the rocks: and these were now lying bound at the dûn, awaiting death.

"Call out my warriors," said Scathach, "and bid all meet at the oak near the Ancient Stones. And bring thither the twenty men that lie bound in the dûn."

There was a scattering of fire and a clashing of swords and spears, when the word went from Maev. Soon all were at the Stones beneath the great oak.

"Cut the bonds from the feet of the sea-rovers, and let them stand." Thus commanded the Queen.

The tall fair men out of Lochlin stood, with their hands bound behind them. In their eyes burned wrath and shame, because that they were the sport of women. A bitter death theirs, with no sword-song for music. "Take each by his long yellow hair," said Scathach, "and tie the hair of each to a down-caught bough of the oak."

In silence this thing was done. A shadow was in the paleness of each viking-face.

"Let the boughs go," said Scathach.

The five score warrior-women who held the great boughs downward, sprang back. Up swept the branches, and from each swung a living man, swaying in the wind by his long yellow hair.

Great men they were, strong warriors: but stronger was the yellow hair of each, and stronger than the hair the bough wherefrom each swung and stronger than the boughs the wind that swayed them idly like drooping fruit, with the stars silvering their hair and the torch-flares reddening the white soles of their dancing feet.

Then Scathach the Queen laughed loud and long. There was no other sound at all there, for none ever uttered sound when Scathach laughed that laugh, for then her madness was upon her.

But at the last Maev strode forward, and struck a small clarsach that she carried, and to the wild notes of it sang the death-song of the vikings.

> O arone a-ree, eily arone, arone!'Tis a good thing to be sailing across the sea!How the women smile and the children are laughing gladWhen the galleys go out into the blue sea—arone!
> O eily arone, arone!
>> But the children may laugh less when the wolves come,And the women may smile less in the winter—cold—For the Summer-sailors will not come again, arone!O arone a-ree, eily arone, arone!
>> I am thinking they will not sail back again, O no!The yellow-haired men that came sailing across the sea:For 'tis wild apples they would be, and swing on green branches,And sway in the wind for the corbies to preen their eyne,O eily arone, eily a-ree!
>> And it is pleasure for Scathach the Queen to see this:To see the good fruit that grows upon the Tree of the Stones.Long, speckled fruit it is, wind-swayed by its yellow roots,And like men they are with their feet dancing in the void air!O, O, arone, a-ree, eily arone!

When she ceased, all there swung swords and spears, and flung flaring torches into the night, and cried out:

> O, arone a-ree, eily arone, arone,O, O, arone, a-ree, eily arone!

Scathach laughed no more. She was weary now. Of what avail any joy of death against the pain she had in her heart, the pain that was called Cuchullin?

Soon all was dark in the rath. Flame after flame died out. Then there was but one red glare in the night, the watch-fire by the dûn. Deep peace was upon all. Not a heifer lowed, not a dog bayed against the moon. The wind fell into a breath, scarce enough to lift the fragrance from flower to flower. Upon the branches of a great oak swung motionless a strange fruit, limp and gray as the hemlock that hangs from ancient pines.

ULA AND URLA[16]

[16] The first part of the story of Ula and Urla, as Isla and Eilidh, is told in "Silk o' the Kine," at the end of *The Sin-Eater*. [The name, Eilidh, is pronounced Eily (*liq.*) or Isle-ih.]

"Rose of all Roses, Rose of all the World! You, too, have come where the dim tides are hurled Upon the wharves of sorrow, and heard ring The bell that calls us on: the sweet far thing. Beauty grown sad with its eternity Made you of us, and of the dim gray sea."

ULA and Urla were under vow to meet by the Stone of Sorrow. But Ula, dying first, stumbled blindfold when he passed the Shadowy Gate: and, till Urla's hour was upon her, she remembered not.

These were the names that had been given to them in the north isles, when the birlinn that ran down the war-galley of the vikings brought them before the Maormor.

No word had they spoken that day, and no name. They were of the Gael, though Ula's hair was yellow and though his eyes were blue as the heart of a wave. They would ask nothing, for both were in love with death. The Maormor of Siol Tormaid looked at Urla, and his desire gnawed at his heart. But he knew what was in her mind, because he saw into it through her eyes, and he feared the sudden slaying in the dark.

Nevertheless he brooded night and day upon her beauty. Her skin was more white than the foam of the moon: her eyes were as a starlit dewy dusk. When she moved, he saw her like a doe in the fern: when she stooped, it was as the fall of wind-swayed water. In his eyes there was a shimmer as of the sunflood in a calm sea. In that dazzle he was led astray.

"Go," he said to Ula, on a day of the days. "Go: the men of Siol Torquil will take you to the South Isles, and so you can hale to your own place, be it Eirèann or Manannan, or wherever the south wind puts its hand upon your home."

It was on that day Ula spoke for the first time.

"I will go, Coll mac Torcall: but I go not alone. Urla that I love goes whither I go."

"She is my spoil. But, man out of Eirèann—for so I know you to be, because [323]of the manner of your speech—tell me this: of what clan and what place are you, and whence is Urla come: and by what shore was it that the men of Lochlin whom we slew took you and her out of the sea, as you swam against the sun, with waving swords upon the strand when the viking-boat carried you away?"

"How know you these things?" asked Ula, that had been Isla, son of the king of Islay.

"One of the sea-rovers spake before he died."

"Then let the viking speak again. I have nought to say."

With that the Maormor frowned, but said no more. That eve Ula was seized, as he walked in the dusk by the sea, singing low to himself an ancient song.

"Is it death?" he said, remembering another day when he and Eilidh, that they called Urla, had the same asking upon their lips.

"It is death."

Ula frowned, but spake no word for a time. Then he spake.

[324]"Let me say one word with Urla."

"No word canst thou have. She too must die."

Ula laughed low at that.

"I am ready," he said. And they slew him with a spear.

When they told Urla she rose from the deer-skins and went down to the shore. She said no word, then. But she stooped, and she put her lips upon his cold lips: and she whispered in his unhearing ear.

That night Coll mac Torcall went secretly to where Urla was. When he entered, a groan came to his lips, and there was froth there: and that was because the spear that had slain Ula was thrust betwixt his shoulders by one who stood in the shadow. He lay there till the dawn. When they found Coll the Maormor he was like a seal speared upon a rock, for he had his hands out, and his head was between them, and his face was downward.

"Eat dust, slain wolf," was all that Eilidh whom they called Urla said ere she moved away from that place in the darkness of the night.

When the sun rose, Urla was in a glen among the hills. A man who shepherded there took her to his mate. They gave her milk, and because of her beauty, and the frozen silence of her eyes, bade her stay with them, and be at peace.

They knew, in time, that she wished death. But, first, there was the birthing of the child.

"It was Isla's will," she said to the woman. Ula was but the shadow of a bird's wing: an idle name. And she, too, was Eilidh once more. "It was death he gave you when he gave you the child," said the woman once.

"It was life," answered Eilidh, with her eyes filled with the shadow of dream. And yet another day the woman said to her that it would be well to bear the child and let it die: for beauty was like sunlight on a day of clouds, and if she were to go forth young and alone and so wondrous fair, she would have love, and love is best.

"Truly, love is best," Eilidh answered. "And because Isla loved me, I would that another Isla came into the world, and sang his songs—the songs that were so sweet, and the songs that he never sang, because I [326]gave him death when I gave him life. But now he shall live again—and he and I shall be in one body, in him that I carry now."

At that the woman understood, and said no more. And so the days grew out of the nights, and the dust of the feet of one month was in the eyes of that which followed after: and this until Eilidh's time was come.

Dusk after dusk, Ula that was Isla the Singer, waited by the Stone of Sorrow. Then a great weariness came upon him. He made a song there, where he lay in the narrow place: the last song that he made, for after that he heard no trampling of the hours.

> The swift years slip and slide adown the steep;The slow years pass; neither will come again.Yon huddled years have weary eyes that weep,These laugh, these moan, these silent frown, these plain,These have their lips acurl with proud disdain.
> O years with tears, and tears through weary years,How weary I who in your arms have lain:Now, I am tired: the sound of slipping spearsMoves soft, and tears fall in a bloody rain,And the chill footless years go over me who am slain.
> [327]I hear, as in a wood, dim with old light, the rain,Slow falling; old, old, weary, human tears:And in the deepening dark my comfort is my Pain,Sole comfort left of all my hopes and fears,Pain that alone survives, gaunt hound of the shadowy years.

But, at the last, after many days, he stirred. There was a song in his ears.

He listened. It was like soft rain in a wood in June. It was like the wind laughing among the leaves.

Then his heart leapt. Sure, it was the voice of Eilidh!

"*Eilidh! Eilidh! Eilidh!*" he cried. But a great weariness came upon him again. He fell asleep, knowing not the little hand that was in his and the small flower-sweet body that was warm against his side.

Then the child that was his looked into the singer's heart, and saw there a mist of rainbows, and midway in that mist was the face of Eilidh his mother.

Thereafter the little one looked into his brain that was so still, and he saw the music that was there: and it was the voice of Eilidh his mother.

And, again, the birdeen, that had the blue of Isla's eyes and the dream of Eilidh's, looked into Ula's sleeping soul: and he saw that it was not Isla nor yet Eilidh, but that it was like unto himself, who was made of Eilidh and Isla.

For a long time the child dreamed. Then he put his ear to Isla's brow, and listened. Ah, the sweet songs that he heard. Ah, bitter-sweet moonseed of song! Into his life they passed, echo after echo, strain after strain, wild air after wild sweet air.

"Isla shall never die," whispered the child, "for Eilidh loved him. And I am Isla and Eilidh."

Then the little one put his hands above Isla's heart. There was a flame there, that the Grave quenched not.

"O flame of love!" sighed the child, and he clasped it to his breast: and it was a moonshine glory about the two hearts that he had, the heart of Isla and the heart of Eilidh, that were thenceforth one.

At dawn he was no longer there. Already the sunrise was warm upon him where he lay, newborn, upon the breast of Eilidh.

"It is the end," murmured Isla when he waked. "She has never come. For sure now, the darkness and the silence."

Then he remembered the words of Maol the Druid, he that was a seer and had told him of Orchil, the dim goddess who is under the brown earth, in a vast cavern, where she weaves at two looms. With one hand she weaves life upward through the grass: with the other she weaves death downward through the mould: and the sound of the weaving is Eternity, and the name of it in the green world is Time. And, through all, Orchil weaves the weft of Eternal Beauty, that passeth not, though its soul is Change.

And these were the words of Orchil, on the lips of Maol the Druid, that was old, and knew the mystery of the Grave:

When thou journeyest towards the Shadowy Gate take neither Fear with thee nor Hope, for both are abashed hounds of silence in that place: but take only the purple nightshade for sleep, and a vial of tears and wine, tears that shall be known unto thee and [330]*old wine of love. So shalt thou have thy silent festival, ere the end.*

So therewith Isla, having in his weariness the nightshade of sleep, and in his mind the slow dripping rain of familiar tears, and deep in his heart the old wine of love, bowed his head.

It was well to have lived, since life was Eilidh. It was well to cease to live, since Eilidh came no more.

Then suddenly he raised his head. There was music in the green world above. A sun-ray opened the earth about him: staring upward he beheld Angus Ogue.

"Ah, fair face of the god of youth," he sighed. Then he saw the white birds that fly about the head of Angus Ogue, and he heard the music that his breath made upon the harp of the wind.

"Arise," said Angus; and, when he smiled, the white birds flashed their wings and made a mist of rainbows.

"Arise," said Angus Ogue again; and, when he spoke, the spires of the grass quivered to a wild sweet haunting air.

[331]So Isla arose, and the sun shone upon him, and his shadow passed into the earth. Orchil wove it into her web of death.

"Why dost thou wait here by the Stone of Sorrow, Isla that was called Ula at the end?"

"I wait for Eilidh, who cometh not."

At that the wind-listening god stooped and laid his head upon the grass.

"I hear the coming of a woman's feet," he said, and he rose.

"Eilidh! Eilidh!" cried Isla, and the sorrow of his cry was a moan in the web of Orchil.

Angus Ogue took a branch, and put the cool greenness against his cheek.

"I hear the beating of a heart," he said.

"Eilidh! Eilidh! Eilidh!" Isla cried, and the tears that were in his voice were turned by Angus into dim dews of remembrance in the babe-brain that was the brain of Isla and Eilidh.

"I hear a word," said Angus Ogue, "and that word is a flame of joy."

Isla listened. He heard a singing of birds. Then, suddenly, a glory came into the shine of the sun.

"I have come, Isla my king!"

It was the voice of Eilidh. He bowed his head, and swayed; for it was his own life that came to him.

"Eilidh!" he whispered.

And so, at the last, Isla came into his kingdom.

But are they gone, these twain, who loved with deathless love? Or is this a dream that I have dreamed?

Afar in an island-sanctuary that I shall not see again, where the wind chants the blind oblivious rune of Time, I have heard the grasses whisper: *Time never was, Time is not.*

Printed in Great Britain
by Amazon